ARCHITECTURAL TREASURES OF EARLY AMERICA

★ ★ ★ ★ ★ ★

EARLY HOMES OF NEW YORK
AND THE
MID-ATLANTIC STATES

ARCHITECTURAL TREASURES OF EARLY AMERICA

★ ★ ★ ★ ★ ★

EARLY HOMES OF NEW YORK AND THE MID-ATLANTIC STATES

From material originally published as
The White Pine Series of Architectural Monographs
edited by
Russell F. Whitehead and Frank Chouteau Brown

Prepared for this series by the staff of
The Early American Society

Robert G. Miner, Editor
Anne Annibali, Design and Production
Jeff Byers, Design and Production
Nancy Dix, Editorial Assistant
Patricia Faust, Editorial Assistant
Carol Robertson, Editorial Assistant

An
Early
American
Society
Book

Published by Arno Press Inc.

Copyright © 1977 by Arno Press Inc. and The Early American Society, Inc.

Library of Congress Cataloging in Publication Data

Main entry under title:

Early homes of New York and the Mid-Atlantic States.

   (Architectural treasures of early America ; v. 6)
(An Early American Society book)
      1.   Architecture, Domestic — New York (State).
2.   Architecture, Colonial — New York (State).   3.   Architecture —
New York (State).   4.   Architecture, Domestic —
Middle Atlantic States.   5.   Architecture, Colonial —
Middle Atlantic States.   6.   Architecture — Middle
Atlantic States.   I.   Miner, Robert G.   II.   Early
American Society.   III.   The Monograph series, records
of early American architecture.   IV.   Series.
NA7235.N7E18   728.3   77-14467

ISBN: 0-405-10069-8 (Arno)   ISBN: 0-517-53271-9 (Crown)
Distributed to the book trade by Crown Publishers, Inc.

CONTENTS

1. New Netherlands Farmhouses   7
   by Aymar Embury, II
   Photographs by Frank Cousins and John Wallace Gillies

2. Manhattan Farmhouses   18
   by Lemuel Hoadley Fowler
   Photographs by Kenneth Clark

3. Eastern Long Island, New York   28
   by William Edgar Moran
   Photographs by Kenneth Clark

4. Rensselaerville, New York   38
   by William A. Keller
   Photographs by Kenneth Clark

5. Cooperstown, New York   50
   by Frank P. Whiting
   Photographs by Kenneth Clark and DeForest Coleman

6. Wood Houses of Central New York   62
   by Carl C. Tallman, AIA
   Photographs by the author

7. Northern New Jersey   72
   by Clifford C. Wendehack
   Photographs and Measured Drawings by Kenneth Clark

8. John Imlay House, Allentown, New Jersey   84
   by John Taylor Boyd, Jr.
   Photographs and Measured Drawings by Kenneth Clark

9. Mount Holly, New Jersey, Court House   100
   by Fenimore C. Woolman
   Photographs and Measured Drawings by Kenneth Clark

10. Eastern Shores of Maryland   116
    by Charles A. Ziegler
    Photographs by Philip Wallace and the author

11. Annapolis, Maryland   126
    by Delos Smith
    Photographs by Pickering Studios

12. "Montpelier," Prince George County, Maryland   142
    by Ward Brown, AIA
    Photographs by Kenneth Clark

13. Early Maryland Houses   158
    by John H. Scarff
    Photographs by Kenneth Clark

14. Wye House   176
    by Elliott L. Chisling
    Photographs by Kenneth Clark

15. Matthias Hammond House, Part I   194
    by Effingham C. Desmond
    Photographs and Measured Drawings by Kenneth Clark

16. Matthias Hammond House, Part II   208
    by R.T.H. Halsey
    Photographs and Measured Drawings by Kenneth Clark

New Netherlands Farmhouses

LONG after the Colonial work of New England and the South became well known to the architects, and had become regarded by them as a suitable source from which to draw precedents for modern work, the remaining examples of the work of the Dutch in their colony of New Netherlands remained unnoticed and neglected. It is not easy to discover why this should have been, since much of it is in close proximity to New York City, some of it indeed within the city limits, and these examples are not inferior in charm, less in number, or of a later date than the Colonial work of Massachusetts and Virginia.

The settlement of New Netherlands antedated by some years that of New England, and its development was steady and rapid, the Colonists pushing out from New York along the river valleys and Indian trails which formed the natural means of communication in a country where roads were still to be constructed. Many of these early Dutch houses still exist, and although the area in which they occur is comparatively small, it must have been, for a farming community, very thickly populated and extremely prosperous. The age of these houses cannot be determined with any real accuracy, and while the earliest of them appear to have been erected about the same time as the earliest remaining examples in New England or Virginia, the very natural tendency to exaggerate the age of old work has probably been not less apparent in New Netherlands than in New England. The whole question of the dates of old work is a rather delicate one, and I have found in all parts of the American colonies that the dates assigned to old buildings were those at which some por-

tions of them had been built, although the entire building might have been reconstructed since that time.

In selecting the subjects for the illustrations for this article, then, I have been unable to find in many cases any real historic evidence as to the dates of construction, and have been obliged to accept family traditions or the records of the local historic societies as guides, and these dates are offered with reserve. The fact is that in most cases the testimony as to the age is probably no better than that given me by a negro employee on one of the old farms, who told me that the house was built "so dog-gone long ago that there ain't nobody remembers when she was built." I have gone into this question of dates with some particularity, because the determination of the sources and progress of any style must rest primarily upon the comparison of houses in their chronological order, assuming, of course, variances in the style arising from local conditions. Now while this evidence is very far from complete, it is convincing on one point, namely, that the Dutch early found their *métier*, and pursued it substantially unchanged up to, and in some cases even through, the period of the Classic Revival. The difference between the earliest of the Dutch houses and the latest is far less marked than the difference between the early and late houses of New England and the Southern Colonies, and without previous knowledge as to the age of the remaining Dutch buildings, it would be practically impossible to pick certain of them out as being the prototypes of the style and others as examples of the style developed.

The most curious thing about the architec-

THE BOARD-ZABRISKIE HOUSE, ON THE PARAMUS ROAD,
NEW JERSEY. Date, 1790, carved in lintel of a cellar window

Note the Chinese-Chippendale ornament in the cornice of
main house. Dormers, wing and railing probably added later

THE BOARD-ZABRISKIE HOUSE, ON THE PARAMUS ROAD,
NEW JERSEY.   Detail of west wing at right angle to road

Of all houses in this section none is more charming; the
interest lies both in the composition and beautiful detail

ture of New Netherlands is that which strikes us in the other colonies, namely, the almost complete renunciation by the Colonists of ideals, processes and precedents of their mother-country. The Dutch houses in Long Island and New Jersey resembled nothing but themselves, and were even more radically different from the work of the Dutch in Holland than they were from the work of the other Colonists. This difference is not alone a question of material, which might be expected in a new country, but is also a question of form and of detail. The steep-pitched roofs of Holland were here transformed into low gentle lines, and the narrow flat cornices of the mother-country were replaced by broad overhanging eaves, from which Classic treatment in general was absent. It was an architecture altogether autochthonous, and not the less interesting for that reason.

The characteristics of the Dutch work are by this time fairly well known: the houses are for the most part one story in height, with low curved overhanging eaves on the front and rear, and an almost total suppression of cornices or rake moldings on the gable-ends. The earliest buildings apparently had single pitched roofs; the gambrel form, so common in these colonies that the term "Dutch roof" has become synonymous with "gambrel," was a thing of later development, although toward the latter part of the seventeenth century it already had become customary; but aside from this one change in the roof shape, apparently the only variation from type was the gradual introduction of a piazza or stoop under the overhanging eaves; and this, too, must

SHENKS-CROOK HOUSE, BERGEN BEACH, FLATLANDS, N. Y. Built 1656

have occurred at a very early date.

The materials in the Dutch work were those used in the other colonies: shingles and clapboards, stone and brick for wall covering, and hewn timbers for the frames. These materials were, however, mingled together with much more freedom than we customarily find in the other colonies, and were perhaps treated with a little better realization of the artistic effect possible from careful selection of materials and appropriate treatment of their surfaces than was elsewhere the case. I do not know of any material used in Colonial times which was so beautifully handled as the red sandstone from which the bodies of many of the houses in Bergen and Hudson Counties in New Jersey were built. The entrance sides of the houses were invariably better finished than the others, and were usually of coursed ashlar with either fine picked or four cut surfaces, small joints and neatly cut sills. The lintels were flat arches, often of wood and with wooden carved key blocks, painted and sanded to represent stone. The other sides of these buildings were of rougher stone or of wood or of brick, handled with a facility and playfulness which in no way detracted from the dignity and attractiveness of the whole building.

We find the same motive in most of the houses still remaining. Each consists of a central mass with one or two wings, invariably placed on the gable-ends, but it is probable that the original houses were single rectangular blocks which now constitute the central portions or in some cases are now the wings, to which the main bodies of the houses have been added.

The materials va-

LAKE TYSEN HOUSE, NEW DORP, STATEN ISLAND, N. Y.

ried with the location: in Long Island the exteriors were of wood, generally white pine shingles but sometimes white pine clapboards; in Staten Island and New York they were sometimes of stone whitewashed or stuccoed, and sometimes of shingles, stone apparently having been used where it was not too hard to cut, and wood used elsewhere. In New Jersey, where the fields were covered with erratic glacial drift of red sandstone, and had to be cleared before cultivation, the bodies of the houses up to the second-story line were generally built of this stone, with the gable-ends, roofs and wings of wood. This red sandstone split readily, was easy to work, and hardened upon exposure to the air, and was therefore chosen in many instances; but it is a curious side-light upon the knowledge of our ancestors to find that people who could work stone so beautifully as the Dutch had no mortar which was durable when exposed to the weather, and the stone walls were therefore protected by overhanging eaves of wood, while the wooden walls needed no such shelter.

The roof shape adopted by the Dutch made dormers unpractical for light in the second story; and as metal for flashing, so essential around dormers, was scarce and difficult to obtain, dormers were usually, if not invariably, omitted, and evidently in those houses which now possess them they were added at a date far later than that of the construction of the main building. The second stories of these houses were therefore lighted at the two gable-ends only, and in several of the old buildings which remain in their original condition I have found that the second-story bedrooms were formed by partitions only, no ceilings having been constructed, so that there was a through ventilation of air from one end of the house to the other over the tops of the bedrooms. The framework was in general constructed in the same manner as in the other colonies: it was of the post and lintel type. In the earliest times the bodies of the walls were built of thick planks set edge to edge vertically; the inner sides of these planks were adzed to give a mortar clinch, and the shingles or clapboards for the exterior were nailed to the outside. The custom of filling in between the posts with studs was probably begun as early as 1725, and the spaces between the studs were often filled with brick or small stone laid up in clay; sheathing was then applied much as it is today, and the outside shingled or clapboarded, although in some instances the buildings were stuccoed directly on the studs and masonry filling between them, without sheathing or lath.

The earlier houses had little interesting detail, and, curiously enough, much of what there

THE BERGEN HOMESTEAD, FLATLANDS, BROOKLYN, N. Y. Built about 1655

THE ACKERMAN HOUSE, HACKENSACK, NEW JERSEY

Date, 1704, carved in end of chimney. Interesting use of columns under the overhang in the center only.

JOHN PETER B. WESTERVELT HOUSE, CRESSKILL, NEW JERSEY.

Date about 1800 An almost perfect example of the full development of the style

THE LEFFERTS HOUSE, BROOKLYN, NEW YORK

Present house dates partly from before 1776 and partly from a century earlier. A portion of the house was destroyed by the British in the battle of Long Island, but was soon rebuilt on its undamaged beams.

THE VREELAND HOUSE,
NORDHOFF, NEW JERSEY

The wing dates from the 18th century;
the body of the house was added about 1825.

THE DOORWAY OF THE LEFFERTS HOUSE ON FLATBUSH AVE., FLATBUSH, L.I. Built in the 17th century, rebuilt about 1780

An extremely interesting doorway, showing the freedom with which the Dutch builders used Classic motives was was strongly reminiscent of Gothic. The doorways, for example, in the old Verplanck house at Fishkill, New York, are not dissimilar from the English Elizabethan type, and hexagonal and octagonal columns were used in very many cases. The later houses, probably through the influence of the New England work, had considerable attention paid to the treatment of the doorways, the cornices and the window openings, and some of the Dutch doorways and cornices are among the most interesting Colonial works still remaining. The cornice of the main part of the Board House (which dates from 1790), has a frieze decorated in the Chinese-Chippendale manner, and the cornice of the wing shows an extremely interesting combination of dentil course and fluting; both cornices are rich, vigorous and refined. Several of the other houses have doorways carved as elaborately as could be done by a carpenter with the tools then at his command; the use of the gouge to form rosettes and other decorated forms being the marked characteristic. An excellent example of this is the doorway of the Vreeland House, which, though late in period, is much more Colonial than Neo-Grec in sentiment.

The Dutch uses of ornament were characterized, however, by the same freedom from traditions as were the masses of their houses; and indeed the pervading sentiment of all the Dutch work is one of spontaneity and disregard for precedent.

The Dutch houses had not, as a rule, very much pretension to stylistic correctness; they were charming rather than beautiful, and quaint rather than formal. This quality makes them especially adapted for precedents for small country houses of to-day, just as the symmetrical dignity of the Colonial work of New England and the South lends itself to larger and more expensive residences which may be termed "mansions."

Certain of the Dutch forms, especially that of the roof, cannot be readily used, the flat slopes of the Dutch work admitting little light and air in the second story; but the other shapes of gambrel, which were used practically all over the United States, and of which there are examples existing at such widely separated points as Castine, Maine; Annapolis, Maryland; and New Orleans, Louisiana, can be harmonized with the spirit of the Dutch work with profit to our architectural design.

ROADSIDE FARM HOUSE NEAR PEARL RIVER, NEW JERSEY

Note the use of "Germantown hoods," and the fact that wings are added to the ends only

THE TERHEUN HOUSE, HACKENSACK, NEW JERSEY.
Date about 1670

The body of the house is the oldest section.   One of the few examples where use
was made of moldings on the exterior other than door and window architraves

THE ROGER MORRIS OR JUMEL MANSION, NEW YORK, N. Y

This beautifully designed doorway is part of the work added during the "restorations" of 1810

Manhattan Farmhouses

ARLY "stranger's in America," those gentlemen who, in former years, came on flying trips and wrote long and uncomplimentary books about the citizens of these more or less United States, made many remarkable discoveries about us. All early travelers without exception noted with a disapproving eye the American country house. Even in recent years one stately and dignified English scholar said while lecturing here, "Your wooden houses, I can't understand. Why don't you put up something in stone and brick that will be solid at the end of three hundred years, as we do in England?" An American to whom the query was put, answered "It is because we don't want that kind of a house. Changes, improvements, new comforts of all sorts come so fast that we don't want a house to last too long. This house is what I want, but not what my children will want. Even I want to make some structural changes every ten years. I can now do it without being ruined, as I could not do in one of your three-century dwellings." "Bless my heart," replied the visitor, "I never thought of that. You want houses that will easily take on improvements as they come, and be free to build a new and better one every generation, if you want to."

While this explanation of the use of wood in building is, to a certain extent, ingenuous, it is,

to say the least, misleading. It does, however, suggest a reason for the small number of Colonial houses of outstanding importance that are still in existence in Greater New York. Each succeeding generation took little interest in the parental home of previous times, and the place more often than not fell into strange hands; was altered, changed, and finally was torn down to make room for some newer manifestation of architectural ingenuity.

There is not, I suppose, a man alive today, who remembers the New York that was, as Henry James said, a "small but promising capital which clustered about the Battery and overlooked the Bay, and of which the uppermost boundary was indicated by the grassy wayside of Canal Street."

At the beginning of the nineteenth century there were on Manhattan Island, not one enormous city, but ten or more comparatively small settlements; each, in all respects, an individual, independent town. The "capital" at the lower end of the island was of course, the most important; but many conditions helped the growth of the other places from time to time. The yellow fever epidemic of 1822, for instance, did more for the fame and for an enlarged population of Greenwich Village—which, even in 1720 had been a town of considerable size—than have even the "villagers" of the present day. At the time of Lafayette's visit to the United States, one citizen informed the visitor at a reception that "I live on Varick Street, in the aristrocratic ninth ward, where all our best families dwell."

Prominent among other settlements were the Bowery Village, Corlaers Hook, Chelsea, Murray Hill, Bloomingdale; and still further north were Manhattanville, Kips Bay, New Harlem, Kingsbridge and others. Each was a town of fair size and each reproduced the essential features of the typical villages of New England. Each had its outlying farms, long tree-lined main street or its village green, its stores, church or churches, its village doctor, blacksmith, etc.

I suppose, in most cases, if one of the original settlers had wandered back to any of these places sixty years ago, that settler would have found it but little changed; possibly a little larger, but in other respects the same. In my own time, however, in the eighteen eighties, when I first began to hunt out what was left of the houses of old New York, if that old citizen had returned Rip Van Winkle-wise, he would have found sad havoc and confusion. Enormous, ugly brownstone "flats" were rearing their galvanized cornices in the air on every hand. The few scattered farm lots that remained seemed waiting in a sullen kind of way for the time when they too should be absorbed in the rush of flimsy Jerry-building.

My recollections of the upper end of Manhattan Island in the eighties are of a place that was neither city, suburb, or country. There were old houses to be found, tumbling down from neglect,

THE TOM PAINE COTTAGE, NEAR THE NEW YORK CITY BOUNDARY

like the Apthorp Mansion, but still, like that place, showing in spite of all neglect, some faint suggestion of their former fine style. Just when the Apthorp house was torn down I do not remember, but the loss of it was a serious one.

You probably remember what Dr. Johnson said about woman preachers—"I told him" said Boswell, "that I had been that morning at a meeting of the people called Quakers, where I had heard a woman preach. Johnson said: 'Sir, a woman's preaching is like a dog walking on his hind legs—it is not done well, but you are surprised to find it done at all.'"

The same thing—but necessarily with some slight changes, it is true, might be said of these few old farm houses on Manhattan Island. Some of them are not given proper care and their preservation has been awkwardly managed, but you are surprised to find them on Manhattan Island at all.

When they were new, and for many years after, these old places were owned by the farmers whose acres stretched out between the two rivers, on both sides of the single highway leading into the "Cittie of Nu Iarck," and the larger ones were the residences of wealthy New Yorkers of that day, who built their "country seats" in the open and undeveloped regions which, at the beginning of the nineteenth century were far from the roaring city that lay between the Bowling green and the new (John McComb's and Joseph Mangin's) City Hall.

Wood, naturally enough, has played an important part in the architectural development of American building. Except during the first years of Dutch predominence, most houses in New York were frame. And even during the days when that influence was still strong, one visitor (Peter Kalm) in 1648 wrote, "The roofs are commonly covered with tiles or shingles; the latter of which are made of the white fir tree, or *Pinus Strobus*, which grows higher up in the country. . . ." etc. The first Trinity church was frame, and going to the other possible extreme of use, so was the first theater in New York. And so, too, was the later Chappel Street theater, a frame building painted—so tradition says—an unbelievably bright red.

Practically all the farmhouses that are to be seen in the City of New York today are of distinct importance as examples of the planning and design of the best types of building erected during widely different periods in the development of Colonial and early Republican architecture.

Two extremely important frame houses are Alexander Hamilton's "Grange" and

THE DYCKMAN HOUSE, BROADWAY, CORNER OF 204TH STREET, NEW YORK, N.Y. Built in 1787

One of four typical New York farmhouses most skilfully restored

DETAIL OF THE ROGER MORRIS
OR JUMEL MANSION, NEW YORK
*One of the original side doors, the only original
exterior door in the house dating from 1765*

the Gracie House. Allan McLean Hamilton in
his "*Life of Alexander Hamilton*" states (page
338) that the "Grange" was "designed by John
McComb, one of the leading architects of the time.

No authority is given by the author for this
statement, and he adds the rather disconcerting
news, to McComb enthusiasts, that "McComb's
excellent work which remains today is the old
City Hall which shows the artistic *influence of
Sir Christopher Wren*," (The italics do not appear
on the original, they are my own) and he adds
a note, more unaccountable still, to say that

THE POE COTTAGE, KINGSBRIDGE ROAD,
BRONX, NEW YORK, N. Y.
*Described during the poet's occupancy as—"so neat, so poor,
so unfurnished and yet so charming a dwelling I never saw."*

"The design was that of Major L'Enfant." This very definite lack of understanding of the entire situation shown by the author of the "*Life*" and evidenced by his confusion of two buildings of entirely dissimilar design, neither of which can be said, even remotely, to show the "influence of Wren," and far distant in their date of erection; would seem to be sufficient ground for questioning his statement of the authorship of the design.

Fiske Kimball in discussing the "Grange" in his recent (and remarkably satisfying) *American Domestic Architecture of the American Colonies and the Early Republic*, apparently accepts McComb's connection as designer of this house on the evidence of the "*Life*." He may, also, have seen in the McComb collection in The New York Historical Society, a plan marked "Hamilton's Country Seat" which I have an indistinct recollection of having seen among the McComb papers. Mr. Kimball adds, also, "that the square headed doorway with side lights, and usually a transom, made their ap-

A GAMBREL ROOF HOUSE IN FLUSHING, NEW YORK, N. Y.
The house dates probably from about 1820

AN EARLY 19TH CENTURY FARMHOUSE AT ELMHURST, NEW YORK, N. Y.
The pediment, semi-circular window, etc., are typical of the first years of the last century

pearance; first, perhaps, in McComb's house for Alexander Hamilton, the 'Grange,' in 1801."

Judging simply from the design, without any documentary evidence, many facts such as the general form of the plan and many of the details give sufficient reason for supposing this house to have been the work of the architect of the New York City Hall.

I use the word "architect" here only after careful consideration, and in the strictest 18th and early 19th century meaning of the word—that of "*one who builds*" or who "*superintends the construction of a building*." It was undoubtedly in that sense, without reference to McComb as having created the design, that the word was used on the cornerstone of the City Hall. The question of the respective merits of the claims for Joseph Mangin and John McComb as designers of the City Hall are discussed at length by I. N. Phelps Stokes in his monumental work on

New York, "*The Iconography of Manhattan Island*."

The Gracie house, in Carl Schurz Park is an extremely fine one in its details, general proportion and design. It is now owned by the City, and is practially in original condition and needs nothing but proper repair and furnishing to make it one of the most popular museum - landmarks of the city.

Archibold Gracie, the builder, was, in his day, one of the most eminent New York merchants, and his house may be considered as an example of the best type of fine country houses of its period. It is just such a fine square building as we would imagine our forefathers to have occupied in the "glorious sea masters days," and like all early New York houses, the location upon which it stands is excellent.

Further uptown, near the northern end of the Island, is the Morris House, which was built, in

1765, by Roger Morris. This gentleman, a colonel in the British army and a staunch Loyalist, found it convenient at the outbreak of the Revolution to remove himself to other parts of the American continent. Washington occupied the estate in 1776.

Various rapid changes followed until the house eventually came into the possession of Stephen Jumel, who modernized the building in many particulars, according to early nineteenth century standards of modernization, and left it practically as it now stands. A few years ago the building was purchased by the city and is now a

The porch columns running through two stories are important documents in the history of Colonial Architecture. Prof. Fiske Kimball, in his articles on *The Study of Colonial Architecture* in *The Architectural Review* in 1918 calls attention to the fact that "No domestic example of the free-standing colossal order has yet been proved to be of pre-Revolutionary date." If the

columns that form the Jumel portico are part of the original building—and there is every indication that they are part of the intention of the original designer—the building is, as far as is known, an almost unique instance of the two story column in American domestic architecture dating from the historically accurate Colonial period.

Rawson W. Haddon in an article on this house, printed in the *Architectural Record* in July and August, 1917, has determined that the house was undoubtedly completed between May and October, 1765. As "a portico supported by pillars, embellished and finished in character" is included in a description of the house in 1791 and as no important changes had been made in the structure between this date and the time that the Morris family left the house, there is every reason to assume the present porch to be a part of the house as it was built.

In discussing the design of this house Mr. Had-

OLD HOUSE AT THE BRIDGE, ELMHURST, NEW YORK, N. Y.

DETAIL OF THE ROGER MORRIS
OR JUMEL MANSION, NEW YORK, N. Y
*A side door, put in place during the
restoration work by Jumel in 1810*

THE ROGER MORRIS OR JUMEL MANSION, NEW YORK, N. Y. Built in 1765
This general view shows the original boarding on the front of the house and the corner quoins. The east side is shingled

don makes a suggestion of no great direct importance in connection with the Morris house, but of distinct interest as an addition to our knowledge of the small details of early history, that "as to design, there would have been no excuse for haphazard method in laying out the building, for architects, if not numerous, were at least not unfamiliar persons in the city. Indeed, in the year of Colonel Morris's marriage, one Theophilus Hardonbrook, who has some excellent designs to his credit, was practicing in the city as "Architect" and in looking for a possible designer for the Morris house it is not stretching the point too far to suggest one or the other of the two gentlemen who announced themselves as architects in the local papers just a month before Morris probably bought the property upon which the house now stands. In the New York *Mercury*, on April 8, 1765, "DOBIE and CLOW, Builders, In Division Street, TAKE this Method of informing the Public, that they undertake to build . . . , after the London Taste. Any Gentlemen who please to employ them, may depend upon having their Work so done, as to bear the nicest Scrutiny. If required they will also give in Plans and Elevations, with Estimates of the Whole, in Squares, Rods and Yards, together with the Quantity of Materials Buildings of any Dimensions will take, in such a Manner as any Gentleman may know his certain cost before he begins to build." While there is no reason to suppose any connection between Dobie and Clow and the Morris house, the employment of an English architect or builder would explain these columns.

William Dyckman's house at 204th Street and Broadway stands on the site of a farmhouse built by his grandfather in 1666 and which was burned during the Revolution. The present house was erected in 1783. If the loss of the earlier building deprives us of a good example of the type of house occupied by the average farmer during the late seventeenth century, it is altogether probable that in its general plan the present building is not entirely unlike the earlier one.

The detail, however, and the appearance of the gambrel roof, and the design of the interior finish show us in all particulars what was usual during the last years of the eighteenth century. This house, still in possession of the Dyckman family, has been restored, furnished with much of the furniture used in the building when it was new, and opened to the public as a museum. The obligation thus bestowed upon the general house building public is a great one. The good that should result from this opportunity of studying an early house properly restored and furnished should dispel much of the confusion about architectural and decorative periods in America, which quite naturally, results from the usual ignorant policy in so-called Colonial Museums of filling rooms with a heterogeneous mass of furnishings covering a period of almost two hundred years and allowing it to be known indiscriminately as "Colonial."

Old country houses and old farmhouses on Manhattan Island are disappearing, and disappearing rapidly, it is true. But many are still to be found in more distant parts of the city. In the Bronx there are many interesting old houses, though none, perhaps, can boast the interest that naturally attaches itself to the tiny Poe Cottage, where the poet lived during the years 1846 to 1849 and where he wrote "Annabel Lee", "Ulaluame" and "Eureka." The little house today looks more nearly as it did in the Poe days than at any time since he left it. During the last few years the restoration of the house has been carried on with great care and is now well on its way toward completion.

In more distant parts of Greater New York the proportion of old houses that have escaped destruction is naturally much greater than in those parts nearer the centers of activity. In Flushing, for instance, among many others, there is the Prince House. The house has so many points of interest, both in plan and design that a carefully measured set of drawings of it would be of distinct interest to the architectural profession.

In Elmhurst, you can find a farmhouse or two if you want to live a farmer's life and still be within the limits of Greater New York.

Daniel Denton wrote of them as early as 1670: "Though their low-roofed houses may seem to shut their doors against pride and luxury, yet how do they stand wide open to let charity in and out, either to assist each other, or to relieve a stranger."

Detail of Porch.
THE WEBB HOUSE, EAST MARION,
LONG ISLAND.

Doorway Detail.
THE ANNA HALSEY HOUSE, WATERMILL,
LONG ISLAND.

THE JOHN HOWARD PAYNE HOUSE, EASTHAMPTON, LONG ISLAND. Built *circa* 1660.

Eastern Long Island, New York

L ONG ISLAND, first outlined by Adrien Block in 1614, stretches out like a long finger between the Sound and the Ocean. Throughout its length it is practically level, except for a small area of rolling hills on the Sound side. The Island is peculiar in that, whereas the north and south sides are fertile, the centre is an almost barren waste covered with scrub oak; only here and there is the land under cultivation.

The settlement of Long Island was divided between the Dutch and the English. The Dutch came from Manhattan and made their first settlements in 1635. The first deed on record is from Governor Wouter van Twiller, and is dated 1636. The English came from Connecticut and the New Haven colonies.

The first English settlement was at Southold in September, 1640; then came Southampton in 1641; and Easthampton, then called Maidstone, in 1649. The colonists soon spread out from these centres and in a short while there was a line of little villages, much as they exist to-day, along the coast and the shores of Peconic Bay and Great South Bay. It is interesting to note that the English settlements, for protection from the Dutch, joined themselves to Connecticut— Southold in 1648 and Easthampton in 1657. It was not until 1664 that the Island was amalgamated with New York.

The earliest houses of which any trace remains to-day are usually of the pitched roof, shingle-sided type, with their various lean-tos and wings, as exemplified by the Mulford and Payne houses at Easthampton and the Mackay house at Southampton, the first dating from around 1660 and the latter from 1700.

The plan of most of the examples is of the straightforward central hall type, with rooms right and left, though there are numerous houses with a side hall, as the front of the house was often devoted to the "best parlor."

Building was almost entirely of wood, with brick chimneys, as stone in most parts of the Island is notably lacking, and the architectural design is correspondingly simple and direct. In almost every example it will be found that the cornice and main entrance comprise the entire architectural embellishment, though now and then a naïve assemblage of roofs, lean-tos and wings lends some semblance of formality to the design. In the neo-classic examples, pilasters, either on the corners, taking the place of the serviceable corner-board, or even distributed across the front, give a greater feeling of architecture to the building, despite the simplicity of the fenestration. The buildings are usually painted white, even the chimneys receiving their

HOUSE AT EAST MARION,
LONG ISLAND.

THE ROE HOUSE,
PATCHOGUE, LONG ISLAND.

HOUSE AT ORIENT,
LONG ISLAND.

HOUSE AT LAUREL,
LONG ISLAND.

HOUSE AT CUTCHOGUE,
LONG ISLAND.

HOUSE NEAR PATCHOGUE,
LONG ISLAND.

THE WEBB HOUSE, EAST MARION, LONG ISLAND.
Built *circa* 1790.

THE WHITE HOUSE, NEAR WATERMILL, LONG ISLAND.

THE MULFORD HOUSE, EASTHAMPTON, LONG ISLAND.
Built *circa* 1660.

coats, a feature that might well be copied on all white houses. The chimney-caps are, either by nature or by art, all provided with black tops.

The materials, as a rule, were oak for framing and White Pine for exterior finish. The construction methods are similar to those in vogue in Connecticut during the same period: oak corner posts and intermediates, sheathed or stripped and covered with hand split shingles, put on with home forged nails.

The unstudied relation of openings to wall-surface and story heights of most of these simple houses seems to make them perfect examples of wooden design. The great simplicity which is their main feature, combined with a naïveté in design, adds to their charm. In no case do we find very grand houses, even the neo-classic examples being human in scale, and it is their utilization as "partis" which is the chief architectural characteristic, giving value to these houses in a work of this kind.

The three little houses on Main Street in Patchogue, the Roe, the Burt and the Robinson houses, are all very much alike in design, the example here shown, the Roe house, having the most interesting doorway, and each having a pleasing side porch covering the extension.

The Livingstone Farm, at Bellport, now the Osborne house, was built about 1802. It possesses unusual detail in cornice, entrance and second story window trim. It is one of the side-entrance plan houses. The Mott house, formerly the Osborne, also at Bellport, retains the original central feature, and, although additions have been made from time to time which have injured the design as a whole, it retains exceptionally interesting detail in porch and railing.

Southampton, one of the earliest settlements, has retained unchanged but few of its old houses; the Mackay house, 1700, being about the oldest. Between Southampton and Watermill is the White house, built in 1849, which shows a development in design and detail of a most interesting character.

Watermill, settled in 1642, has two very good examples, one painted and the other unpainted, both built about 1800. The Thomas Halsey house would be a well-nigh perfect example of the farm-house, were it not for the bay; and the Anna Halsey house, which until quite recently was so surrounded by man-high box as to be almost hidden, has an interesting and very unusual door treatment.

An engaging feature of this country is the presence of windmills, examples of which may be found from Southampton to Easthampton,

THE WEBB HOUSE, EAST MARION, LONG ISLAND. Detail of Doorway.
Built *circa* 1790.

THE OSBORNE (MOTT) HOUSE,
BELLPORT, LONG ISLAND.

THE THOMAS HALSEY HOUSE,
WATERMILL, LONG ISLAND.
Built *circa* 1800.

THE MACKAY HOUSE,
SOUTHAMPTON, LONG ISLAND.

THE ANNA HALSEY HOUSE, WATERMILL, LONG ISLAND.
Built *circa* 1800.

Detail of Doorway.
HOUSE AT EAST MARION, LONG ISLAND.

Detail of Doorway.
HOUSE AT EAST MARION, LONG ISLAND.

and which are of a similar type of construction to the houses, though entirely utilitarian in character.

A perfect quarry of post-colonial remains is to be found on the narrow strip of land lying between the Sound and Peconic Bay, forming the towns of East Marion and Orient, originally Oysterponds. This country was settled in 1649, and the old records tell of houses built in the seventeenth and eighteenth centuries, but no traces of these houses remain to-day to identify them, unless, perhaps, they have been transformed into barns. The supposition is that, with the exception of the Webb house, they have all disappeared. The remaining houses are mostly of the story and a half type, with side or central entrances, and they are so simple that one wonders at the care that must have been spent over the front doors. One little house, here shown, has a perfect miracle of a cornice, delicately fluted, with symmetrically spaced fluted bands, simulating triglyphs, and a cornice termination as unusual as it is ingenious. The Webb house, about 1790, is one of the best precedents for the two story type on the Island. Originally there was a gallery at the second floor level, as shown by the band, and the doorway giving out on this balcony has been replaced, patently, by a window. The entrance doorway has most interesting details, the door being made up of moulded battens, put in on the diagonal, like a barn door. Also, the cap and cornice merit attention, as do the shutters, which open only in the lower half, as the upper sash was fixed.

At Easthampton we have the Mulford house and the home of John Howard Payne, the author of "Home, Sweet Home." These houses, the Mulford and the Payne, built about 1660, are practically duplicates. They are shingled and have low eaves and the cornices are plaster coves. The Payne house is excellently preserved and is a museum of interest. The interiors have panellings which must have been made by a ship's carpenter, so quaintly and delicately are they framed together.

The road from Greenport to Riverhead passes through the towns of Southold, New Suffolk, Cutchogue, Acquebogue and Laurel, all of which have numerous examples of delightful doorways. At Southold, in addition, we find three examples of houses with dormers, a most unusual feature, for practically all the other houses on the eastern end of Long Island have unbroken roofs.

These little wood-built houses display a certain charm and picturesque quality that are not always found in Colonial work of greater pretension. Used as inspiration for modern work of modest character, they are of particular value in enabling the designer to make direct application of their scheme of composition without fear of losing that indefinable individuality which so frequently happens when the larger houses are reduced in scale.

Detail of Cornice.
HOUSE AT EAST MARION, LONG ISLAND.

Doorway Detail.
HOUSE AT EAST MARION, LONG ISLAND.

Built in 1823 by Eli Hutchinson
THE RIDER HOUSE, RENSSELAERVILLE, NEW YORK

Rensselaerville, New York

AFTER climbing some fourteen hundred feet over the high rocky ledge known as The Helderbergs, in the southwestern part of Albany County, New York State, one comes upon a sequestered village—a village not perched upon a commanding hilltop, as one might expect, but half hidden in a sheltered hollow surrounded by wooded hills, and now comprising all that is left of a once thriving and populous settlement.

"On account of the slow growth of the Colony of New Netherlands, the Dutch States were induced, in 1629, to pass an ordinance granting to any member of The West India Company the right of selecting any tract of land, outside of the Island of Manhattan, 16 miles on one side, or 8 miles on either side, of any navigable stream, and extending as far inland as the patroon, (as the proprietor was called) should choose.

The chief conditions imposed were the establishment of a colony of at least 50 persons over 15 years of age, within four years, and the payment of 5 per cent on all trade except that in furs.

Under these grants, Kilean Van Rensselaer, a director in this Company, secured, with additional purchases made through his agents, land twenty-four miles each side of the Hudson, and forty-eight miles inland, constituting Rensselaerwyck, and including what is now Albany County, most of Rensselaer County, and a part of the County of Columbia."

At the close of the Revolutionary War, The Manor of Rensselaerwyck was held by Stephen Van Rensselaer, and then commenced the earliest practicable attempts to settle the more remote parts of it. The Patroon of the Colony, or Lord of the Manor, as he was afterward called, gave to each settler the free use of the land for seven years; and thereafter, if the settler chose to retain it, a perpetual lease or grant in fee, subject to the payment annually of twenty-two and a half bushels of wheat, a day's service with carriage and horses, and four fat fowls, for each lot of one hundred and sixty acres.

To this remote spot, mountainous, stony, and heavily timbered, came sturdy New Englanders— "men in pursuit of labor"—and doubtless they found plenty of it, as the only way of disposing of the forests was to fell, pile and burn the trees upon the land.

The date of the settlement of the village— February 22nd, 1788—is established by a letter written by the son of Samuel Jenkins, the first settler dated February 21st, 1850, in which he says: 'It will be sixty-two years to-morrow, 12 o'clock noon, since my father's family were set off the sleighs in which they were, into a log cabin in this, then a drear wilderness; to look back it appears like a short time, but the difficulties and privations for a number of years will never be forgotten."

The spring brought a party of men looking for farms, and by their united efforts a flouring mill was raised on the banks of the Ten Mile Creek, the ox power of the neighborhood bringing the millstones from the distant village of Hudson.

From this small beginning the settlement grew until in 1832 it was one of the most thriving villages in the state, its position on the post road making it an important stopping place for coaches travelling to and from the western part of New York State. The abundance of hemlock furnished great facilities for leather making. After the roads were in condition for bringing in hides, there were tanneries in every quarter of the town.

Eventually some of these tanneries burned

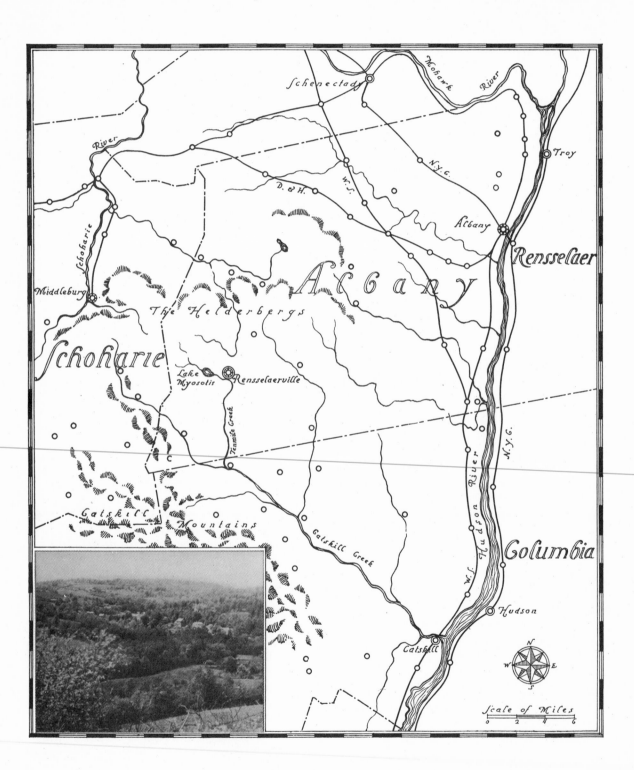

down; the supply of bark was too nearly exhausted to justify rebuilding and so, as seemed inevitable with the advent of railroads in more accessible parts of the state, the prosperity of the village gradually diminished.

The last of its activities ceased with the removal of the woolen mill which had been established there by Messrs. Huyck and Waterbury, and which was for many years one of the few woolen mills in this country.

It is through the interest of the Huyck families that the modern needs of the community have been supplied in the form of a Town Hall and a Library, and through their efforts that many of the old houses have been preserved.

Rensselaerville, as one of the early settlements in the upper Hudson region, has an interest and charm that recall to mind some of the New England villages. The forebears of some of these Rensselaerville families had originally emigrated from Connecticut, becoming pioneers in settling the east end of Long Island, especially at East Hampton, whence came a goodly quota of first settlers to Rensselaerville. Thus the influence of Connecticut architecture can be traced in some of their homes, as shown by their excellent detail and their air of primness.

While three of the houses noted in the article are based on the same general design, each has a distinctive interest. All have a quiet dignity due to their broad fronts, the spacing of windows balancing the enriched central motif of wide pedimented doorway, and graceful Palladian window.

The architect-builder of all but one of the Rensselaerville houses shown in the accompanying photographs was Ephraim Russ. He is mentioned in the chapters on the village history as "that estimable man and faithful builder," and indeed he did faithfully reproduce in these houses the refinement and good taste of New England architecture. That he was engaged in serving his country, as well as his townspeople, is shown by an entry in an 1812 ledger (when the Jonathan Jenkins house was being built) stating that he was advanced, in lieu of money payment, "a regimental coat, do. vest, and military hatt."

GATEWAY OF THE ELDRIDGE HOUSE, RENSSELAERVILLE, NEW YORK

Built in 1806 by Daniel Conkling

THE ELDRIDGE HOUSE, RENSSELAERVILLE, NEW YORK

THE JENKINS HOMESTEAD, RENSSELAERVILLE, NEW YORK

Built in 1809 by Rufus Watson
THE STEVENS HOUSE, RENSSELAERVILLE, NEW YORK

REAR VIEW

The Eldridge house, built in 1806 by Daniel Conkling, is now the summer home of Mrs. Lewis A. Eldridge, the great granddaughter of the original owner. Standing on slightly rising ground, with the reserve naturally given by a low street wall and a white fence, the house looks out over out in this and in most of the other houses illustrated, gives one the impression of a house of greater frontage than forty-eight and one-half feet. The laminated stone of the region provided an excellent material for walls and steps. Screen-doors (themselves a fly in the architectural oint-

Detail of Doorway
THE ELDRIDGE HOUSE, RENSSELAERVILLE, NEW YORK

the village, to the bold outline of the northern Catskills on the distant horizon. The carrying down of the plain surface of the frieze to the cornice of the Palladian window is a feature not usually found in houses of this type. The fine proportion of sash divisions, consistently carried ment!) necessitate in many of these houses a thin shelf in front of the entrance transom bar. The two-story porch at the rear is, of course, a late addition. The immense lilacs along the walk to the entrance are believed to have been set out about the time the house was built.

It is surprising how many taverns and other places for the entertainment of travellers were found necessary, and how large a proportion of the townsmen were indorsed by the Board of Excise as "of good moral character and sufficient intelligence to keep a public tavern." Among those

The original cornice has been restored and a box gutter formed. The original glass, most of which is still preserved, is of a pale green tone.

The Jenkins Homestead, built in 1812, has been occupied continuously by a member of the family ever since that date. There is an old

Detail of Doorway
THE JENKINS HOUSE, RENSSELAERVILLE, NEW YORK

"sufficiently intelligent" was one Rufus Watson, who, in 1809 built and maintained as an inn, the house now the country home of Mr. Clarence W. Stevens. No doubt its broad front, and its hospitable entrance opening almost directly upon the street, invited many a weary traveller within.

letter in which Ephraim Russ (upon being engaged to build this house) writes of his appreciation for having had a free hand in the building of the Daniel Conkling house, and rather laments that he is not to have this same opportunity with the Jenkins house.

The homestead is set back from the street among elms, maples, locusts, black walnuts, and several white pines—one patriarch pine by the roadside standing there as if to show to all passers-by its pride in the old house built of its family stock. The original sash of twenty-four lights have been replaced by those of twelve. This change is regrettably noticeable in the Palladian window, which has the old (false in this case) muntin divisions in the arched head.

The view from the rear shows not only the beautiful setting of trees, but also the great mass of the house, not appreciated by a person viewing it from the street.

In the James Rider house, built in 1823 by Eli Hutchinson, the architectural effect is accomplished by the use of plain members on a wall surface of flush siding, with the slightest projection only, for window casings. The graceful doorway, and the shallow elliptical arches, recall some of the work of central New York State. This is one of the comparatively few houses of this locality that have the gable end toward the street—an arrangement that, in later days, when lots became narrow, and domestic architecture fell to its lowest terms, made the houses on many a village street a saw-tooth row of mediocrities. Ephraim Russ, after completing this house, wrote to a friend that he had been "screwed down to the last cent." And this is by no means the only case in which the architectural

Entrance Detail
THE RIDER HOUSE, RENSSELAERVILLE, NEW YORK

result has been the better because the designer was "screwed down" to a restricted budget!

The Brock Sployd house, built in 1825 by Gurdon Conkling, is a delightful surprise to any one looking in between the quaint old gateposts, and seeing it through the half-screen of foliage. It attracts immediate attention, being so good in proportion and so "correct" in every detail. Its recessed portico of two bays, with a column in the center, is amusing. The average modern architect would say of the designer, respecting the central column, "Why did he do it?" The more—than—average architect would answer "Why shouldn't he do it?" At the left of the porch is an entry; the living room, sixteen by twenty-two feet, extends across the front, and a closet at the right balances the entry. Two gables, slightly separated, form the very unusual side elevation of this unusual house.

The Presbyterian Church, built in 1842, belongs to the Greek Revival period, and, like many others of the time, is essentially carried out along the lines of masonry architecture, though executed in wood. The effect of massive stonework is consistently obtained by the use of flush siding. One regrets the heavy steeple cornices, and that so heavy a moulding was used for the architrave.

The old buildings at the side of the church have all the fifty-seven varieties of width of siding, and

Built in 1825 by Gurdon Conkling
THE SPLOYD HOUSE, RENSSELAERVILLE, NEW YORK

"FENIMORE"—RESIDENCE OF JAMES FENIMORE COOPER, COOPERSTOWN

Cooperstown, New York

THE beauty of the country surrounding Cooperstown has been immortalized in the works of James Fenimore Cooper, eleventh child of William Cooper, the founder of the town which bears his name.

In a letter written some years after his first journey into this forest region of pines and hemlock and green waters, William Cooper describes his lonely venture: "In 1785 I visited the rough and hilly country of Otsego, where there existed not an inhabitant nor any trace of a road. I was alone, three hundred miles from home without food, fire and fishing tackle my only means of subsistence. My horse fed on the grass that grew by the edge of the waters. I laid me down to sleep in my watch coat, nothing but the wilderness around me. In this way I explored the country and formed my plans for future settlement and meditated upon the spot where a place of trade or a village should be established." Evidently from the chronicles written by and of William Cooper, he was a much traveled man, and was more satisfied with the beautiful country around Otsego Lake than with Pennsylvania and New Jersey, from whence he came.

There is a fascination peculiar to this region which one does not find in many places. It is practically away from any main line railroad, midway between the Mohawk River and a valley traversed by the Delaware and Hudson Railroad. For this reason, it has kept to a great degree the old-fashioned spirit both in its manners and customs and in its architecture.

The questions suggest themselves at once how, in a country so far (at that time) from the general lines of travel, such well designed houses were erected and to whom should be attributed their originality. The only record that I can find is of one Hooker, to whom is attributed "Hyde Hall" at the head of the Lake. Possibly the following quotation may shed light on the matter: "During the summer of 1787 many settlers arrived, a good part of them from Connecticut and most of the land on the patent was taken up. Several small log tenements were constructed on the site of the village, and the permanent residents numbered about twenty souls. Meantime, Cooper had been extending his holdings in adjacent patents until he had most of the neighboring country under his control. Toward the end of his life, he had settled more acres than any man in America. It is more than probable that among the settlers from Connecticut and the southern part of New York there were new craftsmen who brought some knowledge of design and building which, if they had no opportunity of showing during their generation, was certainly embued into their descendants."

One may assume that the influence of William Cooper and James Fenimore Cooper was shown as the guiding hand to these craftsmen and their descendants in the design and planning of their houses. I judge this from the beautiful design of Otsego Hall, which is said to have been designed and built by William Cooper in 1799. No doubt these men, whose tastes were of the finer kind, took as much pride in the appearance of their homes as they did in the polish and finesse of their writings. Otsego Hall, (judging from the model now in the village library), was a very pretentious home for those times, and in fact might far surpass many present-day houses of the same size. Its dignity of exterior and proportions cannot be criticized.

This region, at the time of the building of many of the early houses, abounded in the finest growth of virgin pines, growing to great heights and of ample diameters for all building purposes. This, together with a native stone which quarries like elongated brick, and other quarries at the head of the Lake, where hard limestone was plentiful, must have thrilled even the humblest craftsman in his line to make and fashion from these wonderful native materials, mouldings and forms and combinations which grew more pretentious and refined as house succeeded house. Note that in all the illustrations shown, there is not one design identical with another. Many have the same outline and slope of roof, but are varied so that each has individuality.

In 1769 Richard Smith from Burlington, New Jersey, traveled up the Hudson to Albany, thence along the Mohawk Trail to Canajoharie, thence to Cooperstown. His journal, also, contains many interesting incidents relative to Otsego County: "24th: Rained again. The elevated hills of this country seem to intercept the flying vapors and draw down more moisture than more humble places. . . With three carpenters felled a white pine tree and began a canoe. . . Some trout were caught this morning 22 inches long. . . And I approached near to one rabbit whose face appeared to be of a blac color. 25th: We finished and launched our canoe into the lake. She is 32' 7" in length and 2' 4" broad."

The carpenters in those days doubtless were more than willing workers, for, judging from the journal, from the 24th to the 25th they finished a canoe 32 feet long. However, strange as this may seem, the easy working of this soft wood might make such a thing possible. I have seen the most clear-grained planks, soft and of a color like rich cream, some 24 inches wide and 3 to 4 inches thick, come from some of the local sawmills. Through the thoughtfulness of the Clark family, who now own a majority of the woodlands surrounding the Lake, the cutting of these and other trees has been stopped, so that a great deal of the virgin woodland remains.

The homes and houses of a village or community show more than all else the character of the inhabitants and they remain unspoken histories of their builders, for in those times men built their own houses under a guiding craftsman. Without some interesting incident or history connected with each, its individuality is lost, and it becomes simply a good-looking house.

In 1769 Clinton's army camped near the Sus-

"FENIMORE"—ONE-TIME RESIDENCE OF JAMES FENIMORE COOPER, NEAR COOPERSTOWN

THE ROBERT CAMPBELL
HOUSE, LAKE STREET,
COOPERSTOWN, NEW YORK
Built in 1807

THE OLD OTSEGO COUNTY BANK, COOPERSTOWN, NEW YORK
Built in 1831.

"WOODSIDE HALL,"
COOPERSTOWN, NEW YORK
Built in 1829

HOUSE AT OAKSVILLE, FOUR MILES FROM COOPERSTOWN, NEW YORK

quehanna River, at its source, and it was here that the Clinton Dam was built which was to hold back the waters of Otsego Lake until they should be released to allow the boats containing the troops and supplies to be carried some number of miles down the river. Upon the encampment site was built in 1790 what is now the oldest house still standing in Cooperstown. It was built by one Benjamin Griffen. The porch, with its Victorian detail, was probably added later. This house is in perfect repair, very livable and of charming proportions.

The old Otsego County Bank, built in 1831 and now known as the Clark Estate Office, occu-pies a position adjacent to the site of the Grogan hut, one of the first dwellings erected when Cooperstown was a straggling settlement. The Greek portico, with its beautiful two-storied columns, entablature and pediment, is of white pine, in perfect proportion and excellent detail.

At Oaksville, a hamlet of two or three houses and a country store, about four miles from Cooperstown, we find a house where the Classic order has been used, probably inspired by the Otsego County Bank. Its builder must have been a well-to-do farmer and a man of considerable good taste. The walls are of stone in variegated colors of beautiful hues, laid at random with

THE GRIFFEN HOUSE, COOPERSTOWN, NEW YORK

Built in 1790

THE PRESTON HOUSE, COLLIERSVILLE, NEW YORK
Built by Col. Alfred Mumford in 1827

THE PRESTON HOUSE,
COLLIERSVILLE, NEW YORK
Built in 1827

"HYDE HALL"—ON
OTSEGO LAKE,
SEVEN MILES
FROM COOPERSTOWN

wide white joints. Except for the blinds and casings, none of the woodwork has ever been painted, a practice characteristic of the Cooperstown region. The pediment and columns are without embellishment, deriving their undoubted beauty from exquisite proportions and from the soft weathered color of aged white pine so evident even in the illustration. Altogether, this is a most interesting and unusual old house. Besides its architectural charm, it has a melancholy beauty that carries a hint of tales of ghosts and of witchcraft.

Interesting, not only architecturally, but also historically, is "Fenimore," the one-time home of James Fenimore Cooper, famous chronicler of Mohican legends and lore. It is not in Cooperstown proper, but on the shore of Otsego Lake, and is still in the possession of the present James Fenimore Cooper. Sometime after his marriage, the writer moved into Otsego Hall, in the village. "Fenimore" has undergone a change that is detrimental to its otherwise quaint and pleasing character—the porch overlooking the lake is a later and not too well considered addition. The slender columns of the main façade, the simple pediment and the old-fashioned downstairs kitchen, however, are typical of the houses of the comfortably-off farmers of the region and period.

Quoting an interesting incident that occurred shortly after Cooper lived at "Fenimore": "While alterations were in progress at Otsego Hall, Cooper had as his guest Samuel F. B. Morse,

the reconstruction of the Hall and drew designs which gave it more the style of an English country house. The local gossips said that Morse aspired to the hand of his friend's eldest daughter. Cooper had no mind to yield so fair a prize to an impecunious painter, a widower and almost forty-three; Morse was at this time experimenting with the telegraph instrument which was afterward to bring him wealth and fame as an inventor

"TIN TOP"—GATE LODGE OF "HYDE HALL"

"HYDE HALL"—AT THE HEAD OF OTSEGO LAKE, SEVEN MILES FROM COOPERSTOWN

and to overshadow his reputation as an artist."

The Worthington Homestead, on Main Street, built in 1802, was known at that time as "The White House." It differs greatly in style from any of its neighboring contemporaries. Interest in Greek forms as precedents for American domestic architecture was at its height in 1830— this house had embodied the best forms of the Revival a quarter of a century earlier than did many houses built elsewhere and for this reason "The White House" of Cooperstown is unique.

"A country house of classic poise and symmetry was designed in 1829 when Eben B. Morehouse purchased a few acres from the Bowers estate, on the side of Mt. Vision, at the point where the old state road made its first turn to ascend the mountain, and there erected the dwelling called 'Woodside Hall.' For many years an Indian wigwam stood on the site now occu-pied by 'Woodside.' This old stone house, set on the hillside against a background of dense pine forest, has an air of singular dignity and repose. Standing at the head of the ascending road which continues the main street of the village, 'Wood-side,' with its row of columns gleaming white amid the living green of the forest, may be seen from almost any point along the main thorough-fare of Cooperstown.

"A President of the United States was once lost in the grounds of 'Woodside.' It was in 1839 when Judge Morehouse gave a large evening re-ception for President Martin Van Buren. After the reception, when the guests had departed, Mr. Van Buren and a friend who accompanied him became separated from their companions, and lost their way in attempting to find the gate tower. For a long time they wandered and groped about in the darkness of the grounds, finally re-

"THE WHITE HOUSE"—WORTHINGTON HOMESTEAD
MAIN STREET, COOPERSTOWN, NEW YORK *Built in 1802*

THE LYMAN HOUSE, COLLIERSVILLE, NEAR COOPERSTOWN, NEW YORK
Detail of one of the three entrances.   Built in 1816

THE LYMAN HOUSE, COLLIERSVILLE, NEAR COOPERSTOWN, NEW YORK
Built in 1816

turning to the house for a guide and a lantern, just as the family were going to bed."

The columns and entablature of "Woodside" are beautiful in detail and execution and are probably the most perfect in scale of any in Cooperstown. The columns are reeded and terminate in graceful Ionic capitals. Reeded columns seem to have been used frequently in this locality, a treatment quite as effective as fluting. The doorway is of later design, and, as seems to be true of all later additions to these stately houses, is not as interesting as the rest of the house.

Taken as a whole, "Woodside" is a particularly happy example of what can be achieved from a well designed combination of wood and stone.

Seven miles from Cooperstown at the head of Otsego Lake, and half a mile from both the east and the west roads around the Lake, is "Hyde Hall." In all America there is no more unique country-seat. The estate is entered through a gate house, called "Tin Top" because of its gilded tin dome surmounting the arched opening which connects two small, charming cottages. Some distance beyond, at the foot of a wooded hill, "The Sleeping Lion," is the house. The original house was completed by native workmen in 1815. Seventeen years later it was enlarged and a huge hall, with a dining room on one side and a drawing room on the other, was added. The workmen undoubtedly lived in or near the house while it was building, as all the work, from quarrying the stone to cutting and sawing the logs for doors and windows, must have been done on the premises.

The spirit of the true English manor house pervades the entire place, and is maintained in the interior. The main hall as I remember is paved with stone and there ascends from it a circular staircase of solid mahogany. The woodwork throughout the adjoining rooms is also of mahogany, and over the stately mantels are portraits in oil. The long halls and alcoves, the paved courtyards and the old-time kitchens, with cranes and spits, are in perfect keeping. Much might be said of this grand house, and many interesting stories told in connection with it if space would permit.

George Clark, the builder of "Hyde Hall," was the grandson of George Clark, Colonial governor of New York from 1737 to 1744, and inherited a portion of his grandfather's vast estate in Cooperstown.

"When Ambrose Jordan began the practice of law in Cooperstown, he planted an elm tree on Chestnut Street, in front of his house, at the northwest corner of Main Street. This elm, grown to mighty proportions, celebrated its one hundredth birthday in 1913. Within a few paces of the corner, facing on Main Street, and in the rear of the dwelling which fronts Chestnut Street, stands the small building that Jordan occupied as an office. This is one of the few remaining examples of the detached law offices which were common in Cooperstown, as in other villages, in early days, and often stood in the dooryard of a lawyer's residence, apart from the dwelling."

Robert Campbell, of the well-known Cherry Valley family, built for his residence, in 1807, the house that still stands on Lake Street; one façade, overlooking an old-fashioned garden, commands a beautiful view of the lake. The proportions of the house are pleasing; its cornice is ornamented by a row of triglyphs, exceptionally refined in detail. This treatment is also repeated over the windows.

All these dwellings which were built in Cooperstown in the late 18th and early 19th Centuries remain today to perpetuate the spirit of the region. As a rule, the old wood-built houses have outlived the stone ones. This may be attributed to the fact that the lime mortar has given way where exposed to frost and rain.

In conclusion, let me say that if the introduction of the Mansard roof and ugly brick fronts with arched windows had never pervaded Cooperstown, we would still have a village where both the commercial buildings and private dwellings were in perfect harmony.

END DOORWAY
THE LYMAN HOUSE,
COLLIERSVILLE,
NEAR COOPERSTOWN, NEW YORK

THE MILLER HOUSE, LUDLOWVILLE, NEW YORK.

Wood Houses of Central New York

IN the year 1828, prior to which time almost all of the post-Colonial buildings in Central New York had been erected,—for the Greek revival had then begun to assert itself,—a gentleman from Scotland, one James Stuart, accompanied by his wife, passed through this section upon the first leg of a three-years' tour covering most of the parts of the United States then inhabited. To the author Mr. Stuart's narration of stage-coach episodes and his description of the villages of Central New York seem to create an atmosphere of the early days which hardly could be equalled by a present-day writer. Ninety years ago the villages must have presented a chaste and dignified appearance, unspoiled by motley groupings of almost all the known styles of architecture and "carpentecture" which in later years were planted heterogeneously amidst the unassuming post-Colonial structures. Probably the simple character of the villages was not greatly disturbed by the Classic revival, which held sway until about 1845, although the de-

signers of that period aimed at more pretentious edifices. Their work, however, failed to possess that subtle charm which the earlier builders had managed to incorporate in their structures. It is not necessary to dwell at length upon the horrors that succeeded the decline of the Greek revival and the lack of appreciation of the old work which became manifest when so-called "modern" improvements were introduced. Suffice it to say that from the author's observations the post-Colonial buildings of Central New York have suffered more at the hands of "progress" than have those in any other section of the country.

Let us then go back to the early days, taking our seats upon the stage at Utica in company with our narrator:

MAP OF CENTRAL NEW YORK.
Showing James Stuart's Route.

From 30th of August to 1st of September, 1828. From Utica to Auburn.

"We found the stage partly filled before we prepared to take our seats,—half an hour before sunrise,—and did not reach Auburn until nearly

REAR PORCH.

Photograph by Owen F. Scott

HOUSE AT VERNON CENTER. NEW YORK.

sunset. The morning was very hot, but we had some welcome showers in the forenoon, after which the heat became much more tolerable, the road indifferent, and frequently not in the best line; but our charioteers drove pretty steadily at the rate of seven miles an hour. There were many wooden bridges over creeks,—the name given to small rivers in this country,—and the rapid driving of our cumbersome machine down the hills to those bridges was at first rather appalling; but the drivers got on so fearlessly, and at the same time seemed to have their horses so well in hand, that we very soon thought ourselves as safe as in an English stage coach. Our route led us through hill and dale. much land, all cleared and settled within the last thirty or thirty-five years.

HOUSE AT VERNON CENTER, NEW YORK.

We passed villages, — t o w n s we should call most of them: New Hartford, Manchester, Vernon, Oneida, Lenox, Chittenango, Manlius, Jamesville, Onondaga, Marcellus, and Skaneateles, adjoining a lake of the same name. The valley of Onondaga is exceedingly beautiful, and the town neat and clean looking, with a handsome opening and piece of fine sward in its centre. We were in the neighborhood of two small settlements of Indians. In one place, the children of the Indians followed the stage a long way to get a few cents from us. Everything has a thriving appearance in this district—crops good —and we have also to-day seen many patches of buckwheat. Farm-houses, generally with a portico, piazza, or balcony on one side, and a few locust trees or Lombardy poplars about the

HOUSE ON WEST SIDE OF SKANEATELES LAKE, NEW YORK. Built circa 1818.

buildings, and in all cases large orchards at this season laden with fruit. Near the house, and sometimes in the orchards, is the burying-ground of the family, marked by the erection of a few grave-stones.

"We breakfasted at Vernon, seventeen miles from Utica, this morning, and had even more than an abundant American breakfast set before us. Onondaga is the usual place for dining on this journey; but a party of militia on duty there had, I presume, partaken of our dinner; for we were told that we must wait for some time. This we were unwilling to do; and, having got a lunch of cheese and bread, we delayed our chief meal until we reached the coffee-house hotel.

"Auburn itself is situated on the outlet of the Oswesco Lake, conveniently for manufactures,

THE HOWARD SOULE HOUSE,
Sennett, Cayuga County, New York. Built 1814.

and is a thriving place, with a population of about 4000. It might have been the Auburn of Goldsmith, but for its numerous manufacturing establishments, and for its being the situation of one of the two great state prisons of the State of New York. There are printing offices, and various newspapers here, as at all the villages; one of the papers devoted entirely to religious discussion and intelligence. There are several hotels; one of them, a splendid-looking house, contains about 200 beds.

"Nowhere in this country has there been a more complete change since the revolution, than in that part of it where we are now travelling, in point of general improvement of population, and the comforts of living and travelling."

"Soon after our visit to the Auburn prison, we left the very comfortable family hotel at that village in the stage for Ithaca, at the head of the Cayuga Lake, in order to have a look at the village of Aurora, on the eastern side of the lake, and to see a little more of the lakes than we should if we had adhered to the direct western road, which passes the outlets or northern ends of those lakes. The lakes are parallel to each other, about thirty-three or thirty-five miles long, and two miles broad; our route is by the eastern side of the Cayuga Lake to Ithaca, and thence by the western side of Seneca Lake to Geneva on its northern extremity.

"We proceeded by the western road as far as the outlet from Cayuga Lake, where there is a wooden bridge remarkable for its length, above a mile, and thence by the east side of the lake to Aurora, which is charmingly situated on rising ground above the lake, and is considered an eligible place of residence, on account of the beauty of the surrounding scenery, and cheapness of the necessaries of life. The village does not consist of a connected street, or rows of houses, but a number of detached, clean-looking, and apparently comfortable small villas, inclosed in courts, or spots of garden ground ornamented with a few weeping willows or locust trees.

"We passed many good farms, some of them recently brought into cultivation, on which the usual processes of house-building, and inclosing by strong wooden rails, were in progress.

"Ithaca is a very flourishing village, of between 3000 and 4000, and buildings in rapid progress.

"We pursued our journey on the 5th towards Geneva. The only village we passed on our way to Geneva was Ovid, with its handsomely situated church, and fine piece of green turf between the church and hotel. The American villages are generally announced to you by the spires of their churches peeping through the trees.

"The situation of Geneva on a terrace above the lake is very delightful, as well as commanding, and the village, containing some good houses, and a population of 2000 or 3000, seems an agreeable place of residence, more cheerful looking, and the landscapes and views more pleasing, than any of our resting places since leaving the vale of the Mohawk.

"Early on the 7th September, we proceeded to Canandaigua, on the lake of the same name,

HOUSE AT ELBRIDGE, ONONDAGA COUNTY, NEW YORK.
Built circa 1815.

THE PHELPS HOUSE, NORTH MAIN STREET, CANANDAIGUA, NEW YORK.
Detail of Side Elevation.   Built circa 1813.

HOUSE, 544 SOUTH MAIN STREET, GENEVA, NEW YORK.
Built by Dr. Mandeville, 1800–1818.

THE BOODY HOUSE, ROSE HILL ON SENECA LAKE.
Opposite Geneva, New York. Built circa 1835.

HOUSE ON SOUTH MAIN STREET, GENEVA, NEW YORK.
Built in 1820 by Charles A. Williamson.

THE BALDWIN HOUSE, SOUTH STREET, AUBURN, NEW YORK.
Built circa 1838.

THE THOMAS BEALS HOUSE, NORTH MAIN STREET, CANANDAIGUA, NEW YORK.
Built circa 1815.

sixteen miles distant from Geneva, through a very fertile district; it is considered the most beautiful village in the State of New York; population about 3000. It rises gradually for above a mile from the lake, with an extensive opening for the public buildings in the centre of the street. I am not sure, if I admire the situation more than that of Geneva, but the style of the houses is decidedly superior. There is more appearance of their having been designed and set down with taste than I have ever observed elsewhere. In short, advantage has been taken of the ground, and of its relative situation with the lake, to place them on the fittest spots. They are generally separate and distinct dwelling-houses, their exterior painted perfectly white, and they recede from the street of the village, the sides of which are shaded with trees, inclosed in neatly laid out gardens. Some houses are large, and too good to be denominated villas."

Having caught a glimpse of the country and the principal villages as they appeared ninety years ago, let us rapidly retrace our journey in order to observe the present condition of the old houses. A careful survey to-day points out two facts very clearly. First, where roofs have been maintained reasonably weather-tight the old buildings invariably are found to be as sound as ever. Second, where their charm has been appreciated,—and consequently their original appearance preserved free from serious alterations,—the early houses stand out as examples of domestic architecture worthy of becoming the source of inspiration for modern home-builders. Instances of such appreciation are to be seen in Canandaigua and Geneva perhaps to a greater extent than in other villages and cities, although here and there throughout the territory are to be found scattered examples which have been spared. No architect—in fact,

no layman, if he possesses an interest in such matters, and it is evident on the whole that the layman's appreciation is continually increasing —should miss the opportunity of visiting Geneva and Canandaigua when he is in their vicinity. No guide is needed to point out the delightful old houses in these towns, but in the remainder of the territory the tourist must travel many miles always with his eyes wide open,— for the interesting examples of early architecture are not always apparent to the casual observer. The interest of such a tour, however, is not confined to architecture, for the country in the vicinity of the Finger Lakes, with its combination of natural scenery and well-developed farms, is wonderfully beautiful.

The oldest houses are to be found mostly on or near the original turnpike. Colonel Williamson (whose house at Geneva is illustrated herein) is authority for the following in reference to the road from Utica, via Cayuga ferry and Canandaigua, to the Genesee River at Avon: "This line of road having been established by law, not less than fifty families settled upon it in the space of four months after it was opened." Though the road was probably laid out in 1794, it seems not to have been constructed for some time, for in June, 1797, Col. Williamson represents the road from Fort Schuyler to the Genesee as little better than an Indian trail. It was, however, so far improved subsequently, that on the 30th day of September, 1799, a stage started from Utica and arrived at Genesee in the afternoon of the third day, and from that period it is believed that a regular stage has passed between these two places. In the year 1800, a law was enacted by the legislature of the State for making this road a turnpike. The work of construction was commenced without delay, and completed in a short time.

THE Dr. CARR-HAYES HOUSE, GIBSON STREET, CANANDAIGUA, NEW YORK. Built 1826.

THE GRANGER HOUSE, NORTH MAIN STREET, CANANDAIGUA, NEW YORK.
Front Elevation.   Built circa 1816.

TWO HOUSES ON MILL STREET, ITHACA, NEW YORK.

THE TERHUNE HOUSE, ANDERSON AVENUE, HACKENSACK, NEW JERSEY

Built by John Terhune about 1670

THE ACKERMAN HOUSE, POLIFLY ROAD, HACKENSACK, NEW JERSEY

Northern New Jersey

THE early architecture found in New Jersey, more particularly on the banks of the Hackensack River, stands apart and distinct from all other types of early American domestic architecture in the United States.

These houses with their quaint gambrel roofs, wide overhanging eaves and broad flat walls of brown stone, have usually been designated as "Dutch Colonial" although this term is incorrect and misleading.

The best examples of the style peculiar to northern New Jersey were erected long after 1664 when Manhattan Island and the surrounding country had ceased to be a Dutch Colony. The style developed slowly, reached maturity in the beginning of the eighteenth century, and attained its highest perfection after the War of Independence.

There is a type of true Dutch Colonial architecture, found in South Africa in the Dutch and Boer settlements which was developed when the veldt was still under Dutch rule. It is a very simple style with low broad walls and simple openings, but it never attained the charm and proportion of the style developed in America.

The Dutch descendants who settled in northern New Jersey, had very little intercourse with their English neighbors to the south in the region of Philadelphia. Living in an isolated manner, these hardy northern settlers expressed in their homes their tenacious individuality, and for several generations adhered very closely to a set type of plan and design. Whether their houses were large or small the same characteristics can be seen in all the work done in this section.

The history of this particular portion of New Jersey along the banks of the Hackensack River, from the town of Hackensack to the New York State line, is most interesting particularly that bearing on the houses under consideration.

The Delaware Indians, among whom was a tribe called the Hackensacks, caused the early settlers considerable trouble, and it was not until the last quarter of the seventeenth century, about 1670, that John Berry an Englishman, and a French Huguenot named Demarest, were each granted an extensive tract of land, comprising what is now the town of Hackensack and the surrounding country. This tract was soon occupied by Dutch settlers from Manhattan. Records bear the date of 1686 when these settlers began to unite into community life, and the beginning of the next century found many prosperous communities of busy farmers with the Dutch habits of thought and expression.

With this element, mingled the French Huguenot strain, descendants from the Demarests, which, however, never became strong enough to dominate the Dutch influence.

Slavery was introduced in New Jersey in 1664, and the land owners were encouraged to increase the number of slaves by a bonus of seventy-five acres of additional land for each slave brought into the colony. Records show that in Bergen County alone there were twenty-three hundred slaves in 1790. This fact has a very important bearing on the architecture of this period, for, being possessed of unlimited, inexpensive labor, the Dutch tendency towards solidity could be indulged in to the utmost. The stone used for the walls of their houses, was in all probability cut and laid by slave labor.

The stone employed is usually called brown stone, and is to be found in great profusion throughout New Jersey. In many localities this brown sandstone is found in ledges and was easily adaptable to the solid flat beds so characteristic of this early masonry.

Stone of irregular size laid in random bond was used generally until the beginning of the nineteenth century when it became a practice to employ cut stone for at least the front and corners with uniform jointing which produces a modern effect in some of the later examples.

The Demarest House is one of the most effective illustrations of highly developed stone work. On the rear and ends is demonstrated the earliest type of bonding and irregular laying of stone, and by observation it will be seen that the horizontal beds are maintained throughout in a most exacting manner.

There is abundant proof that practically all of this early masonry was originally laid in ordinary clay taken from the surrounding fields and mixed with straw. The quality of the New Jersey soil was particularly adapted to this use. Stone work laid in red clay mortar was practically impervious to moisture, and many examples of

clay joints in window sills are still intact. At later periods of restoration, most of this stone work was pointed up with lime mortar producing the white joints.

The most characteristic feature of these houses is the enormous overhang and sweep of the eaves. Undoubtedly the Dutch thrift of maintaining property without repairs was responsible for the development of this very charming construction, as it was the means by which water was diverted from the walls of the buildings and prevented the washing out of the clay joints in the masonry.

Assuming that this theory of the overhanging eaves is correct, it is not easily explained why the gable walls were made so extremely flat, in fact, more so than in any other type of early American architecture. However, there was some thought taken to the condition of the gable walls by the fact, hardly without exception, that the gables were covered with shingles and later with clapboards. Thus for purely utilitarian reasons there was developed one of the most charming architectural compositions.

The overhanging roofs were sheathed on the under side with boards and were usually carried out to form a boxed cornice five or six inches deep on the outer edge. On the gable ends a delicately moulded skirt border was generally used and occasionally a small row of dentils is to be found.

When the original cottage grew too small for its

THE HOPPER HOUSE,
POLIFLY ROAD,
HACKENSACK,
NEW JERSEY

Built during the years 1816-1818

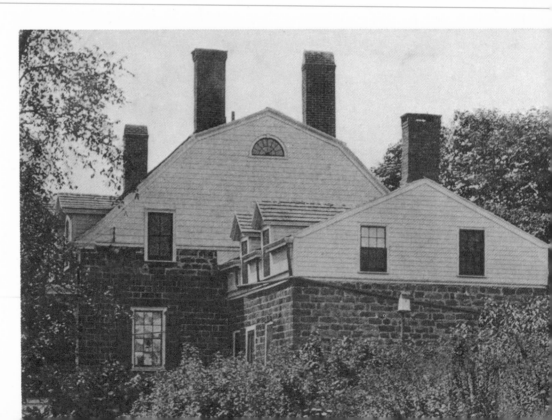

THE KIPP HOMESTEAD ON THE BANK OF THE HACKENSACK RIVER

Built circa 1800

owner, a second larger house was built against one end, and in most cases became the main portion of the house and the original building was often changed into a kitchen wing. Frequently a second wing was added to balance the original house. Thus the form of plan so often found was the result of natural growth of the size and prosperity of the family.

A reversed order of building is found in the Terhune House in Anderson Street, Hackensack, New Jersey. The main portion of this house, which is built of brown stone and now white-washed, was built by John Terhune in 1670. In 1800 a descendant of the original owner occupied the house and added a frame wing for kitchen and dining room use.

Irrespective of the period in which the earliest por-

tions of these houses were constructed, there seems to have been a faithful adherence to tradition as to lines and roof pitches which has created an exquisite mass so characteristic of the region. The steeper slope is slightly less than forty-five degrees and the top slope ranges from twenty to twenty-three degrees and is usually quite short.

Around a tradition which permitted in the beginning only the use of local sand stone, many interesting variations in architectural forms employing the native pine are to be found. One of the most interesting is the employment of square wood columns. The original excessive overhang was transformed into a porch and undoubtedly many of the examples, where these narrow columned porches are to be found, were added to at a later date.

The Kipp Homestead on the banks of the Hackensack River is one of the most interesting examples left to us both historically and architecturally. In the gabled end facing the river, we find an example of the natural tendency of these builders to employ masonry wherever possible. We are told that the bricks in this wall were brought from Holland by an early Dutch trader as ballast. The opposite gable is of clapboards; the front and rear walls are surmounted by a most unusual cornice of delicately carved modillions.

Toward the beginning of the nineteenth century, the treatment of doorways, cornices and window openings were given added consideration as may be seen in the Vreeland House. Note the clever use of one and the same set of mouldings throughout and to see what rich and vigorous carving was done with a gouge.

The Lincoln House in Hackensack, originally built by an uncle of John Terhune in 1773, is an excellent demonstration of the softening effect of round pine columns and the more abundant use of wood cornices and gables made possible by a modern restoration of the original sand stone house. The cornice, details and roof lines have been faithfully carried out from the original.

To appreciate these old homes of New Jersey at their best, one must view them in their native landscape amid the rolling slopes and green meadows which have formed their setting for so many generations.

The mellowing effect of time and the elements has brought out the texture of the stone work and in many cases the original wood clapboards or shingles have been left to us without paint, and have mellowed to a golden russet as may be seen on the gable end of the Ackerman House on Polifly Road, Hackensack.

It would be a noble work indeed if the New Jersey State Board of Architects could acquire some of these finest examples and preserve them intact without mutilation for posterity.

END ELEVATION—THE DEMAREST HOUSE ON THE SADDLE RIVER, NEW JERSEY

Built in 1837

REAR ELEVATION—
THE DEMAREST HOUSE
ON THE SADDLE RIVER,
NEW JERSEY

Built in 1837

THE JOSEPH C. LINCOLN HOUSE,
HACKENSACK, NEW JERSEY

Restoration of the original house built
by an uncle of John Terhune in 1773

END ELEVATION—THE VREELAND HOUSE, NORDHOFF, NEW JERSEY
Built in 1818

DETAIL OF FRONT ELEVATION

THE VREELAND
HOUSE

NORDHOFF, NEW JERSEY

MEASURED DRAWINGS *from*
The George F. Lindsay Collection

THE VREELAND HOUSE,
NORDHOFF, NEW JERSEY

Front Doorway

THE VREELAND HOUSE,
NORDHOFF, NEW JERSEY

Built about 1818

THE VREELAND HOUSE, NORDHOFF, NEW JERSEY
Detail of Front Doorway

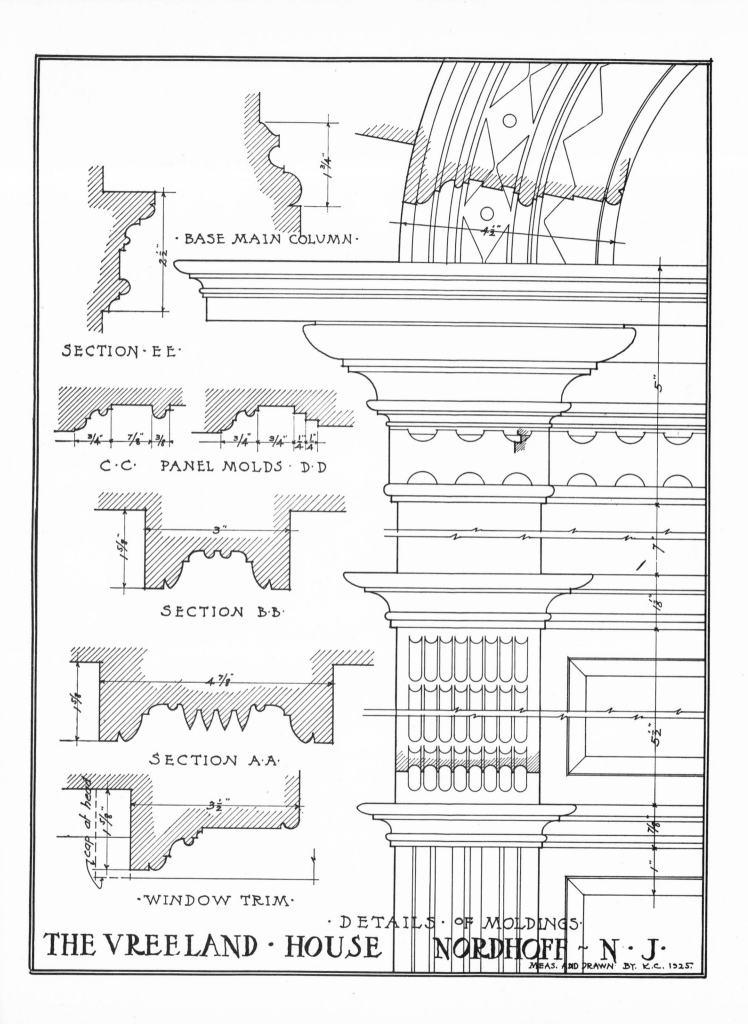

· BASE MAIN COLUMN ·

SECTION · E·E·

C·C·   PANEL MOLDS · D·D

SECTION · B·B·

SECTION · A·A·

· WINDOW TRIM ·

· DETAILS · OF · MOLDINGS ·

THE VREELAND · HOUSE   NORDHOFF ~ N·J·

MEAS. AND DRAWN BY. K.C. 1925.

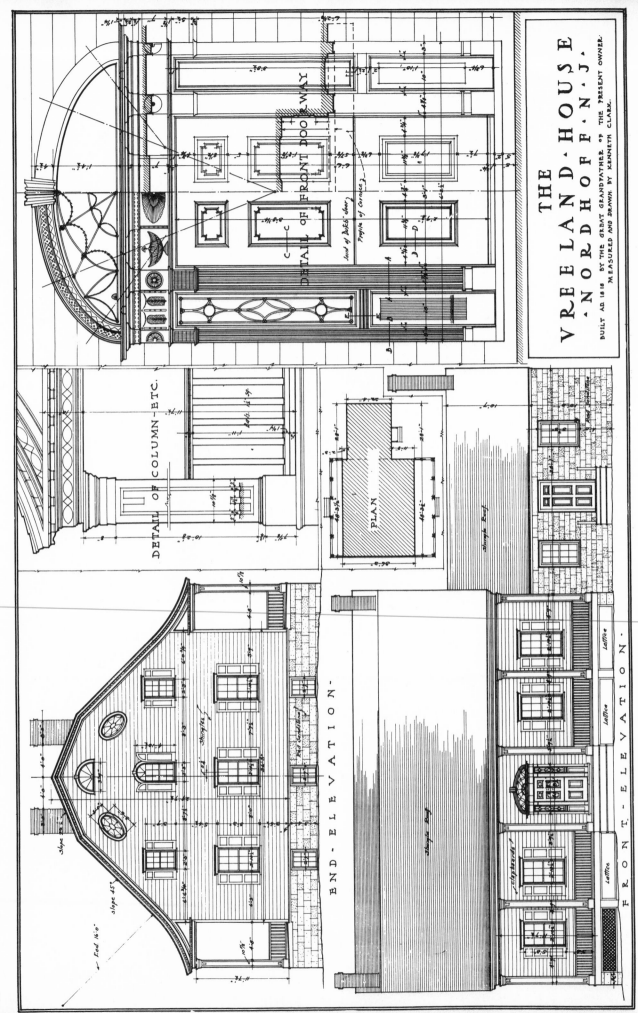

THE
VREELAND·HOUSE
·NORDHOFF·N·J·

BUILT AD 1818 BY THE GREAT GRANDFATHER OF THE PRESENT OWNER.
MEASURED AND DRAWN BY KENNETH CLARK.

DETAIL·OF·FRONT·DOOR·WAY

DETAIL·OF·COLUMN·ETC.

PLAN

END·ELEVATION·

FRONT·ELEVATION·

NUMBER 220 GRAND AVENUE, ENGLEWOOD, NEW JERSEY   *Built in 1803—the oldest house in Englewood*

THE HENDRICK BRINCKERHOFF HOUSE, TEANECK, NEW JERSEY

PARLOR *Mantel*

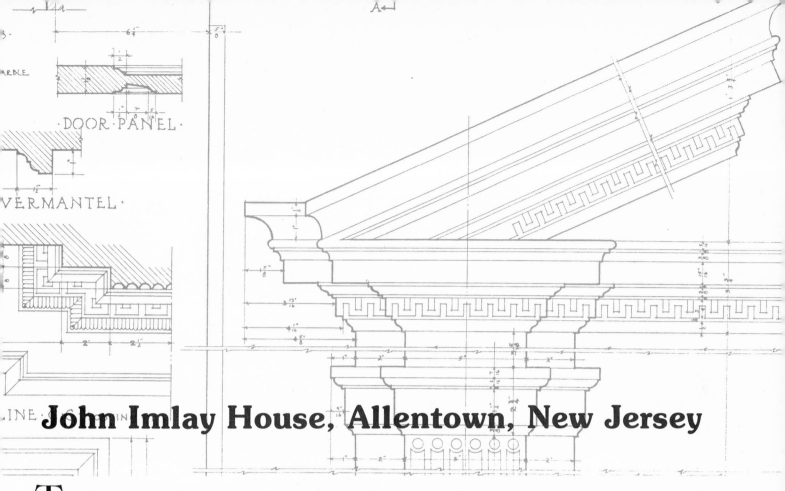

John Imlay House, Allentown, New Jersey

THE RARE QUALITY of the Imlay House, and particularly the extraordinary interest of its interior, deserve to make it widely known. Among the many Early American houses remaining in New Jersey, this house has scarcely a rival and it would take high rank among old houses outside the state.

Connoisseurs of Early Americana know of the Imlay House as the source of the wall-paper now in one of the rooms of the American Wing of the Metropolitan Museum of Art, New York. Architects who are familiar with our native tradition doubtless have noted the brief mention of the Imlay House made in the excellent book, "Colonial Architecture for those about to Build," by Wise and Beidleman. But such mention is entirely too scant; only those few who have actually seen the house itself have any idea of its distinction.

Nor is there much knowledge available concerning the Imlay family. John Imlay (b. 1754–d. 1813), who built the house, was a shipping merchant engaged in the West Indies trade, with offices in Philadelphia, but who retired to the placid countryside of New Jersey for his permanent home. The writer has a slight knowledge of the Imlays, since his grandmother was an Imlay, whose father, Robert Imlay, was likewise a prosperous Philadelphia merchant, closely related to the Imlays of Allentown. Another Imlay was Gilbert, captain in the Continental Army, who, after the Revolution, went to Paris and there entered into a love affair with Mary Wollstonecraft, the English writer and pioneer feminist, whose daughter married the poet Shelley.

The date of construction of the house must fall close after 1790, because the bill of sale for the wall-paper now at the Metropolitan Museum, bears the date of April 18th, 1794. The paper was sold by William Poynsett of Philadelphia, a well known maker and importer of wall-papers. It is an imported French Louis XVI, hand blocked, classic design, in a pattern of light grey garlands and small medallions displayed against a reddish-brown background, delicate in scale.

In those days of the first decade of the Republic, Allentown consisted of about three substantial houses built in a group close to the elm-lined road, and in addition a gristmill that was situated about two hundred yards away. Allentown lies ten miles east of Trenton and about forty miles northeast of Philadelphia. The Trenton district was important at that time and Jerome Bonaparte made his first residence in America at Bordentown, six miles away from Allentown. Today, Allentown has changed but little from the idyllic days following the Revolution. It has grown to about a score of houses and the old gristmill still runs! Requiescat!

The Imlay House is placed lengthwise of the road and is brought so close to the street line that the lowest of the four marble entrance steps encroaches on the sidewalk. The two short, balanced wings are set back, permitting a small lawn closed off from the street by a picket fence. The corners of the house are placed to the four cardinal points of the compass. The plan of the main house is the familiar one of an entrance opening from the street into a central stair hall running entirely through the house, with four main rooms, two on each side. These main rooms, about twenty feet square, are formed by a transverse wall and the two big chimneys are placed back to back, to serve the front and rear rooms.

One of the wings is the kitchen and the other was John Imlay's office. Each has a chimney in the gable end. The house is abundantly supplied with open fireplaces, there being eleven all told, each one furnished with a mantel, and each mantel different in design from the others. The more important rooms are variously decorated with low wainscot, fine door and window trim and ornamental cornice at the ceiling.

The house is solidly constructed, having stone foundations that are carried nearly up to grade, topped with several courses of brick, forming a low base which is finished with a moulded brick watertable. The interior division walls of the cellar are of brick.

The main house and the wings are roofed with ridges running the long way of the house. The main roof is pierced with three small gabled dormers, placed close to the eaves and designed with arched windows and small pilasters. Except for a small porch which has been added to the kitchen wing, the house remains today practially unchanged.

Such are the main characteristics. It is when one examines the carefully wrought, classic detail that one sees what a masterpiece it is, this serene old home of the Early Republic. Conventional as the exterior is, one could never tire of its simple, frank proportions. It is trite to say that every line, detail and moulding is right and could not be changed without damage to the effect, but it is true in this case. The broad low proportions,

the perfect scale of the two rows of windows, the delicately detailed cornice and above all the beautiful doorway, with its jewel-like sparkle of decoration—these can hardly be over praised.

The architectural elements of the Imlay house, are fairly typical of the period and of the region northeast of Philadelphia. Every bit of detail, down to the tiniest curve and moulding has been studied almost to the ultimate possibility of craftsmanship. As a result of this exceptional design and workmanship, the Imlay House is like one of those finest masterpieces of Early American furniture—say one of Duncan Phyffe—which has a final touch of grace, of perfection beyond other similar pieces.

The shutters are thicker and have more character in the panel mouldings than is usually the case. On the main doorway, the delicate play of light and shade on its projecting forms reveal much subtlety that is not at first apparent. Note in the illustration the tiny drill-holes accenting the vertical channelings and the under sides and front of the dental course under the raking cornice, also the wood pattern of the fanlight with the three little "drumsticks" in the centre, and the moulded edge of the door jamb, which is stopped by a tiny block just below the impost of the arch.

The main cornice shows the same imagination and the same infinite care. The edges of the clapboards and of the gable are beaded, in order to soften the lines; the vertical corner-board is panelled and is more strongly modelled than usual; and the graceful brackets under the overhanging cornice have an unusual detail, particularly at the corner. The details of the dormers are slightly more accented, in order, no doubt, not to lose their character when seen from the street. Another variation is seen in the change in size of the window panes on the ends of the main portion of the house and in the wings. On the front, it will be noticed that the siding is matched in order to present a more finished surface close to the street. This siding has a $\frac{1}{4}''$ bead and is about $5\frac{5}{8}''$ wide. The end clapboards are laid about 8″ to the weather.

But, as I have intimated, remarkable as the exterior of the Imlay House is, even more interesting is its interior.

The interiors have all the sophistication and fine finish of the best early Republican houses of the mansion type, as found in the north. They have not the low-ceilinged, homely air of the farmhouse type on the one hand, nor have they the Georgian massiveness of the great Southern plantation homes. They seem to stand midway

Detail of Cornice

OFFICE WING

DETAIL OF UPPER STORIES

Detail of Dormer Window

Detail of Window and Shutters

89

DOORWAY

between these extremes. Indeed, John Imlay's house bears much resemblance to the homes of his contemporary merchant ship masters of Salem and Newburyport and, in detail, one senses the same classic hand in the work of the craftsmen or architects who built this house —probably men from Philadelphia—as one feels in the Salem interiors of Samuel MacIntyre.

In all, the house contains fifteen rooms, of which the most important naturally are those on the ground floor of the main portion of the house. It is a curious fact that the interior cornices have almost the same design as the cornice of the exterior, although their scale, of course, is smaller. Points of interest are the original tile fireplace facings in the two main front rooms and the hardware, of which the locks are generally the box-lock type, of wrought iron with brass handles.

The detail of the main stair hall has a touch of farm house architecture, though it is quite perfect in the design of rail, balusters and stairs. An unusual form is the graceful scroll-saw ornament under each riser.

One could hardly imagine a finer interpretation of the style than is seen in the decoration of the drawing room. This work is indeed comparable to MacIntyre's, and it was here that just a little more effort was spent, if possible, than in the others. Its rare beauty is attained by scholarly design, by the rich details and by the same painstaking workmanship that is noted throughout. This is apparent in the illustration of the detail of the upper part of the over-mantel, showing the room cornice. The parlor is less sophisticated, particularly with regard to the cornice, than the drawing room, but it is no less perfect and has a charm of its own. John Imlay's portrait hangs over the mantel.

Upstairs, one finds a different treatment in the guest room of the second story front. The cornice is heavier and the detail has more relief. The mantel is almost square in shape to fit the smaller fireplace of a bedroom and it does not extend across the full width of the chimney-breast, but leaves a space for a row of long panels on each side. The original wallpaper is still on the walls. It is of a freer design than the one in the Metropolitan Museum, but equally delicate and finished with dark border at the top under the wood cornice.

There is an endless fascination about an old home like this. Its quiet beauty is typical of the Early Republican days of serenity and good living. Our age is different but perhaps this very fact makes us appreciate all the more a fine example of the admirable architecture of earlier times, such as the Imlay House.

Detail of Entrance Doorway

LOWER HALL—*Doorway*

Detail of Stair Well

Detail of Newel and Stairs

THE JOHN IMLAY HOUSE
ALLENTOWN, NEW JERSEY

❧

MEASURED DRAWINGS *from*
The George F. Lindsay Collection

❧

DRAWING ROOM—*Mantel*

DRAWING ROOM—
Detail of Cornice and Over-mantel

DETAIL OF MANTEL SHELF

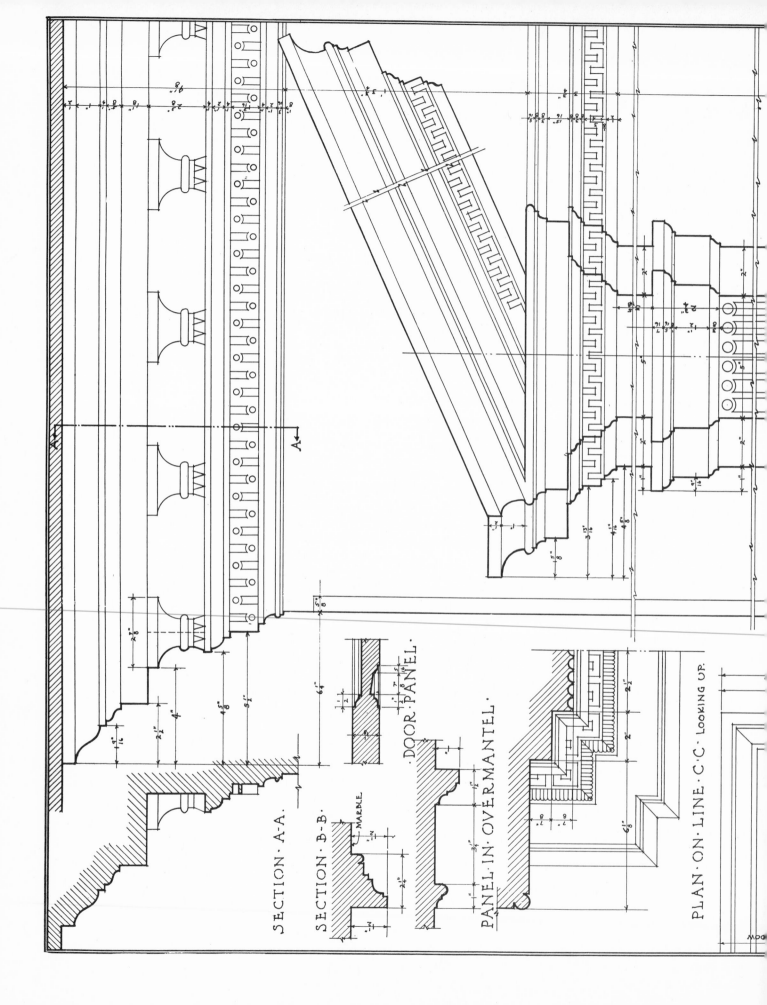

SECTION·A·A.

SECTION·B·B.

DOOR·PANEL.

PANEL·IN·OVERMANTEL.

PLAN·ON·LINE·C·C· LOOKING UP.

MARBLE

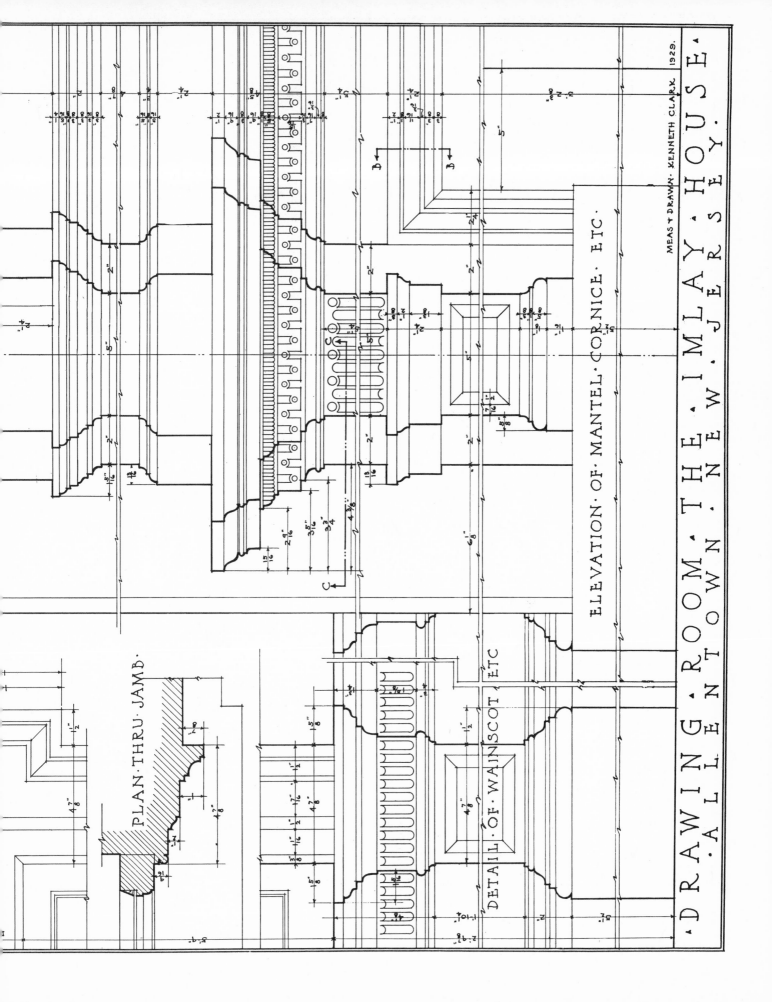

ELEVATION · OF · MANTEL · CORNICE · ETC ·

PLAN · THRU · JAMB ·

DETAIL · OF · WAINSCOT · ETC

· DRAWING · ROOM · THE · IMLAY · HOUSE ·
· ALLENTOWN · NEW · JERSEY ·

MEAS + DRAWN · KENNETH CLARK. 1929.

Detail of Mantel

GUEST BEDROOM *Mantel*

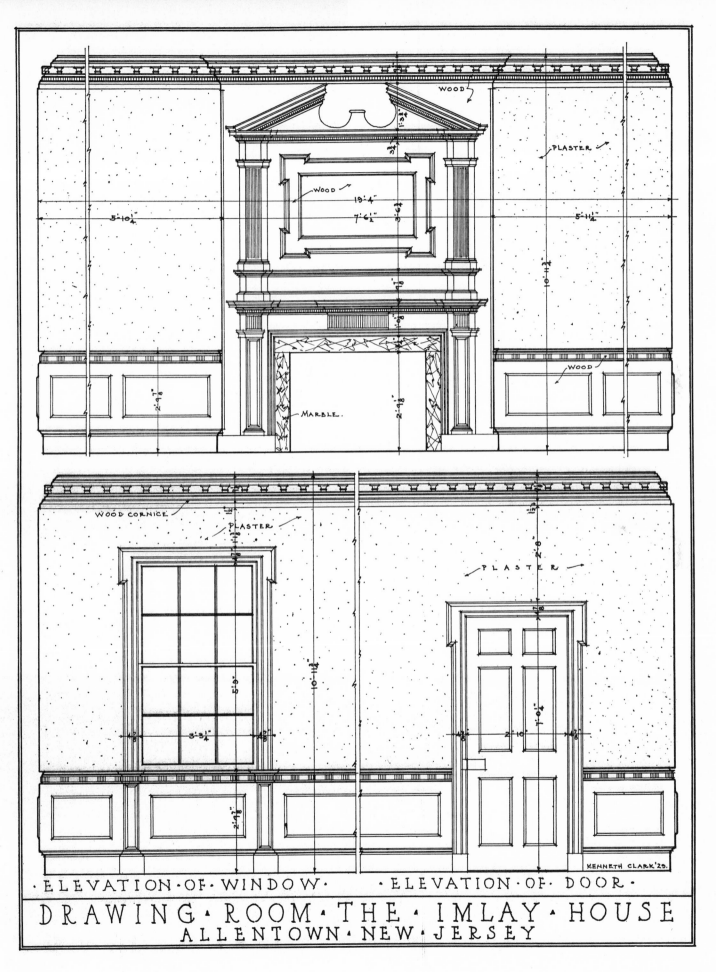

· ELEVATION · OF · WINDOW ·   · ELEVATION · OF · DOOR ·

DRAWING · ROOM · THE · IMLAY · HOUSE
ALLENTOWN · NEW · JERSEY

DETAIL OF MAIN CORNICE

THE BURLINGTON COUNTY
COURT HOUSE,
MOUNT HOLLY, NEW JERSEY

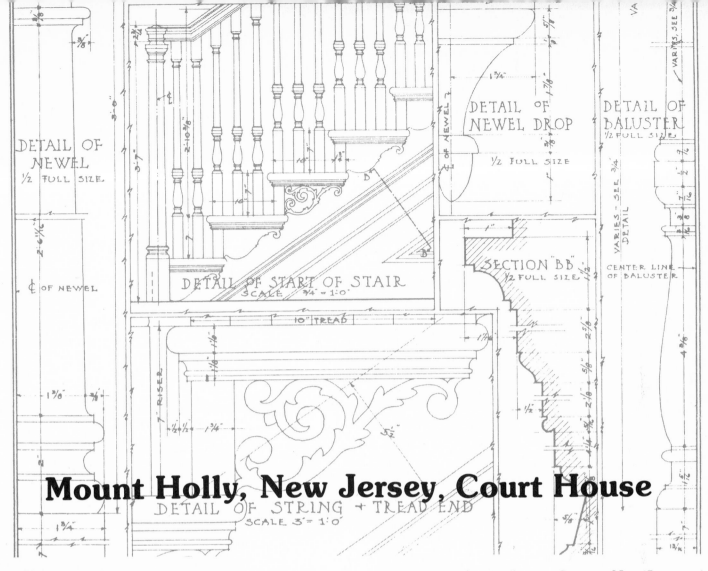

DETAIL OF NEWEL
½ FULL SIZE.

DETAIL OF START OF STAIR
SCALE ¾" = 1'0"

DETAIL OF NEWEL DROP
½ FULL SIZE

DETAIL OF BALUSTER
½ FULL SIZE

SECTION "BB"
½ FULL SIZE

10" TREAD

DETAIL OF STRING + TREAD END
SCALE 3" = 1'0"

Mount Holly, New Jersey, Court House

NSPIRING history often takes place in buildings of inspiring architecture —or inspiring architecture creates an atmosphere condusive to high and ennobling events, as the reader likes. In either case, probably the most famous early American public buildings are the group surrounding Independence Square in Philadelphia, a group composed, you will remember, of the dignified State House, with its arcades and wings, designed by the great amateur architect, Andrew Hamilton, now known as Independence Hall, and the two buildings that complete the group — the Philadelphia County Court House and the City Hall, erected in 1787. Congress sat in the latter building from 1790 to 1800.

In those early days some knowledge of architecture was considered an essential part of every gentleman's education, for at least two reasons; to round out his general knowledge and as a practical tool when the time to build his own dwelling or to assist in the planning of some public building came. The trained professional architect of today was almost unknown. It is not surprising therefore to find that Major Richard Cox, Zachariah Rossell and Joseph Budd, having been entrusted in 1796 with the building of a new County

Court House for Burlington County, New Jersey, should have been able to emulate the creator of the Philadelphia City Hall, its dignity and repose having aroused their admiration, and that they or their appointed craftsmen were successful in catching the spirit of the earlier building and adapting it to their own needs and purposes. The Court House which these amateur New Jersey architects conceived is not as well known to the architectural student of today as is "Congress Hall"—not because they were unsuccessful in their purpose to create a beautiful and well constructed building, but rather because Mount Holly is in a "sand hole" in West Jersey, if we use the geographical term used in the early days, several miles from the old city of Burlington, the first capital of West Jersey, and not on the beaten path of the architectural explorer.

The Court House at Mount Holly, is nevertheless, one of our priceless American architectural inheritances, standing virtually as it was built, an enduring memorial to the most elegant period in early American architectural history. Its very dignity precludes any idea of unseemly conduct or lack of majesty in the administration of the business of meting out Justice— yet it was built only after violent and bitter contention.

According to the records, the original County Court

CORNICE DETAIL—COLLECTOR'S OFFICE

THE BURLINGTON
COUNTY BUILDINGS
COLLECTOR'S OFFICE

THE BURLINGTON COUNTY COURT HOUSE, MOUNT HOLLY, NEW JERSEY

House, which was built in the city of Burlington on the shores of the Delaware River in 1690, was in such a state of delapidation by 1795, that a large expenditure of money was required to repair it, which money the freeholders refused to vote. An act of legislature was passed, enabling the people to erect a new court house, and authorizing a vote of the people of Burlington County to determine where it should be built, as many thought the public buildings should be nearer the center of population than Burlington, which is at one side of the county. The places nominated were Black Horse, Mount Holly and Burlington. Mount Holly won after much excitement and a hotly contested election. Dr. Read, in his "Annals of Mount Holly" says: "I am informed that at the election held at the Mount Holly Market House, to say where the court house should be built, that some voters came from the pine districts with dingy faces, and after voting, retired to the saw mill race, washed themselves, returned and voted again. This may have been true, but for want of proper authentication, we may consider it the product of a romantic imagination and place no reliance upon it." But, such propaganda, evidently rife at the time, had its effect in keeping alive feelings of resentment, however amusing it may be a century and a half later.

The citizens of Burlington were so aggravated by the loss of the court house that it would have been unwise, if not actually unsafe for a Mount Hollian to show himself in Burlington. The indignity of being shorn of their pride was never forgiven or forgotten by the old citizens of Burlington, but now time has healed the wound.

The Mount Hollians being victorious, the court

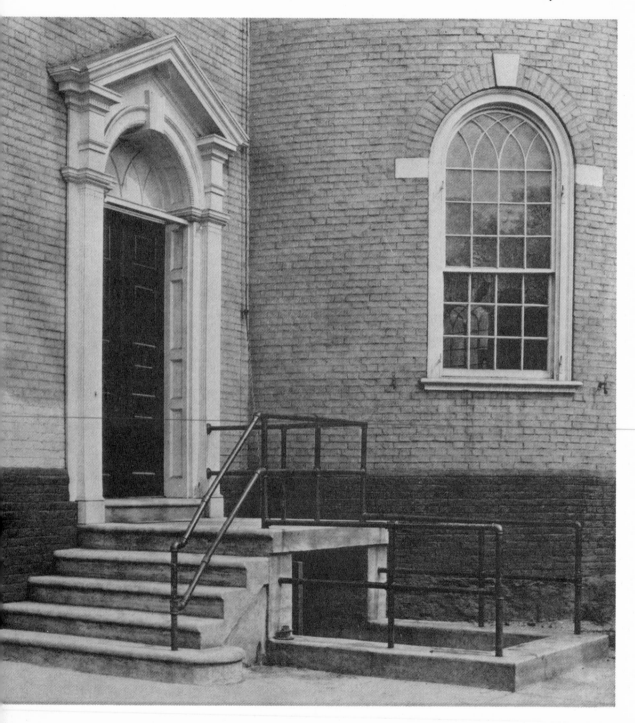

Detail of Rear Entrance Doorway

WINDOW DETAIL—COURT HOUSE

INTERIOR OF COURT ROOM—BURLINGTON COUNTY COURT HOUSE, MOUNT HOLLY, NEW JERSEY

house was erected in 1796 on land purchased in that year from Joseph Powell for 210 pounds. The contracting carpenter for the building was Michael Rush, a native of Mount Holly. Samuel Lewis was a master carpenter and assisted in and superintended the construction. Undoubtedly they were aided in their work by a careful study of the City Hall in Philadelphia and by the early architectural reference books containing measured drawings of Georgian details which appeared in America toward the middle of the eighteenth century.

Like the little building in Philadelphia, the court house is an oblong structure of brick with marble and white wood trim, two stories high, hip roofed and surmounted in the center by a well proportioned octagonal open cupola. On the front a pediment springs from the cornice over a slightly projecting central section of the facade. Unlike the "Congress Hall," in that, instead of a three sided bay breaking the rear wall, it has a semicircular wall to form the end of the court room.

We feel that the "designers" of the Mount Holly building have been more successful in the treatment of the stoop and doorway feature than their brethren in Philadelphia. The simple dignity and scale of the doorway with its graceful fanlight above are in accord with the round headed windows of the lower story. These windows are set effectively in the brick arched openings with marble sills and keystones. Like "Congress Hall," the round topped windows have sliding sash with twelve paned lower sashes and upper sashes with ten small ornamental panes to make up the semicircle above twelve rectangular panes. The upper story windows have twenty-four panes except the one over the entrance, which has thirty panes. They are square headed with flat brick arches and marble keystones.

The brick walls are surmounted by a hand tooled wood cornice, its coved member having a series of recessed arches and the Grecian band or double denticulated moulding beneath. At the second floor level a

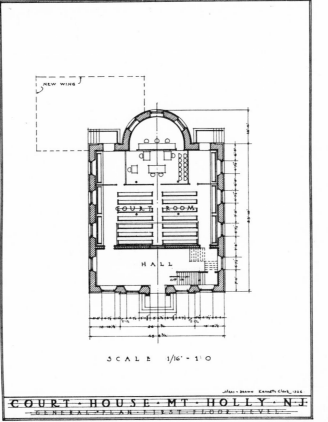

SCALE 1/16' = 1·0

COURT · HOUSE · MT · HOLLY · N·J
GENERAL · PLAN · FIRST · FLOOR · LEVEL

white marble belt course has been used. The coat-of-arms cut in marble and set in the wall over the front door was a later addition, being the gift of one Isaac Hazalhurt.

In 1807 the Surrogate's office to the north and the Clerk's office to the south of the court house were built, making a most attractive group.

No less interesting than the outward appearance is the aspect of the spacious hall with its beautiful staircase with a half-way landing. As originally planned there was a large folding door in the center of the hall, opening into the court room; on each side of the door there was a gallery with seats one above the other for spectators. In the center of the court was a platform elevated some twelve inches above the aisle and surrounded by a high railing with turned balusters of slender grace. The space was used for the grand and petit jurors. The illustration shows the court room as it is today with a rearrangement of the spectators' seats, railing, desks, jury box, etc.

The climb into the cupola from the upper story disclosed the generous roof timbers obtained in the days when Mount Holly was on the edge of the great forest area known as the Pines or Pine Barrens. The old name "Pine Barrens" implies something like a desert but as a matter of fact, the region produced magnificent forest trees. The original growth, pine in many places, consisted also of lofty oak, hickory, gum, ash, chestnut, etc., interspersed with dogwood, sassafras and holly and in the swamps the valuable cedar.

Like the early houses of West Jersey, the Court House at Mount Holly is of simple, well proportioned architecture of a distinctive type, less luxuriant, massive and exuberant than that across the river in Pennsylvania although both were evidently derived from the Christopher Wren school. The old court house seen today in its setting of ancient and still flourishing button-wood trees, seems to reflect faithfully the simple feeling of the Quaker people.

The Burlington County
COURT HOUSE *at* MOUNT HOLLY, N. J.

~~∽∾~~

MEASURED DRAWINGS *from*
The George F. Lindsay Collection

~~∽∾~~

DIRECT VIEW OF FRONT ELEVATION

CUPOLA, COURT HOUSE
AT MOUNT HOLLY, N. J.

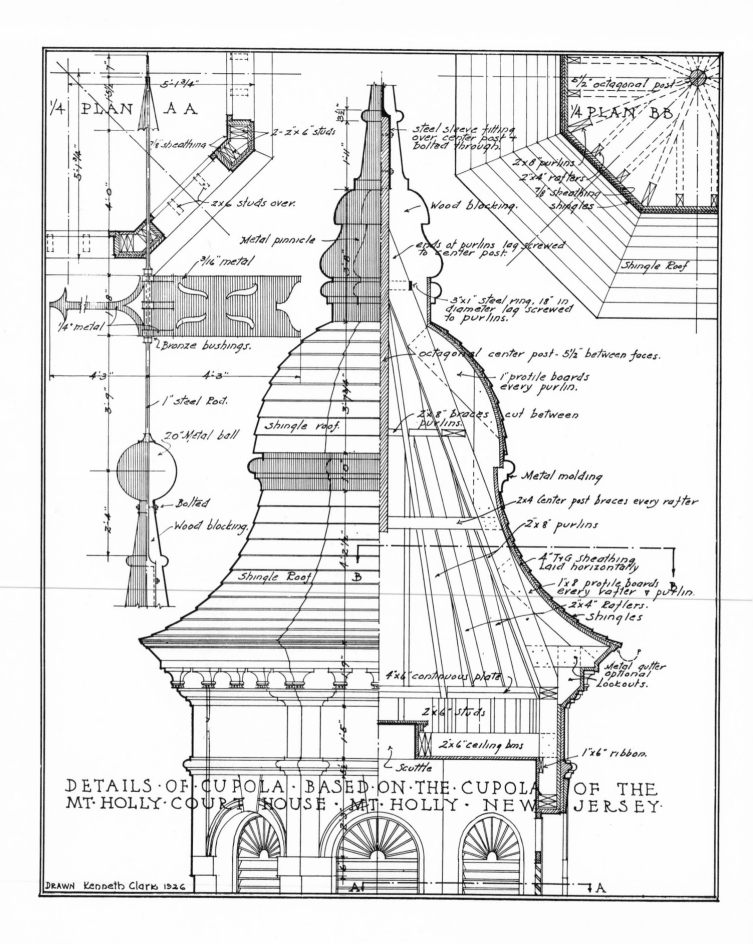

¼ PLAN A A

5'-1¾"

⅞ sheathing

2-2"x6" studs

2x6 studs over.

Metal pinnacle

3/16" metal

¼" metal

4'-0"

5'-1¼"

Bronze bushings.

4'-3"   4'-3"

3'-9"

1" steel Rod.

20" Metal ball

Bolted

Wood blocking.

2'-4"

Shingle roof.

Shingle Roof

B

steel sleeve fitting over center post & bolted through.

Wood blocking.

ends of purlins lag screwed to center post.

3"x1" steel ring, 18" in diameter lag screwed to purlins.

octagonal center post - 5½" between faces.

1" profile boards every purlin.

2"x8" braces cut between purlins.

Metal molding

2x4 center post braces every rafter

2"x8" purlins

4" T+G sheathing laid horizontally

1"x8 profile boards every rafter & purlin.

2"x4" Rafters.

shingles

Metal gutter optional Lookouts.

4"x6" continuous plate

2"x6" studs

2x6" ceiling bms

1"x6" ribbon.

Scuttle

¼ PLAN BB

5½" octagonal post

2"x8" purlins
2"x4" rafters
⅞ sheathing
shingles

Shingle Roof

DETAILS·OF·CUPOLA·BASED·ON·THE·CUPOLA·OF·THE
MT·HOLLY·COURT·HOUSE·MT·HOLLY·NEW·JERSEY·

A'   A

DRAWN Kenneth Clark 1926

110

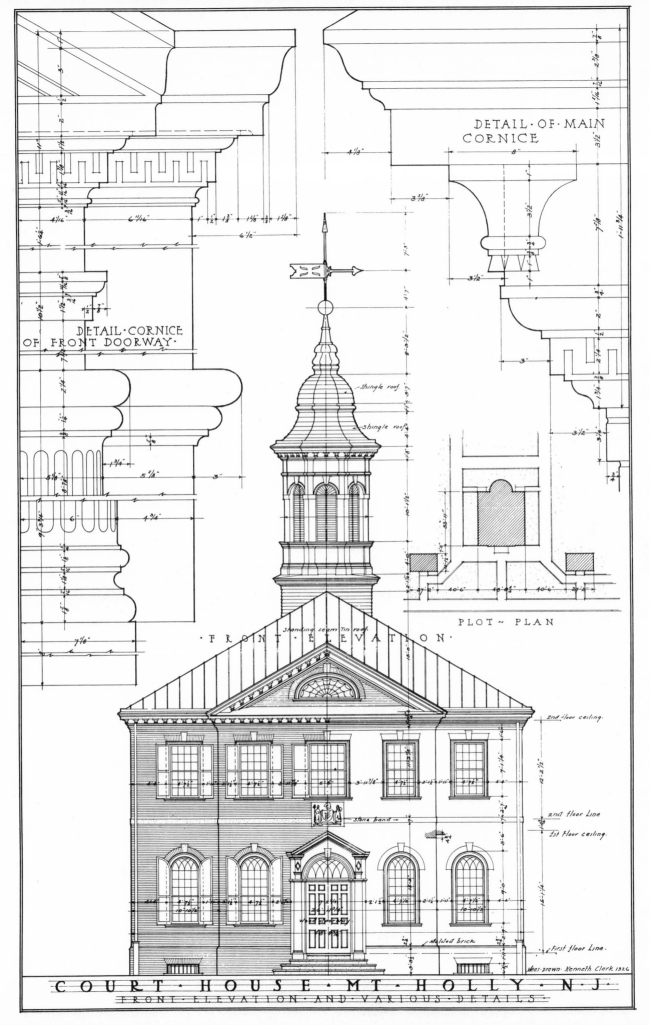

DETAIL·OF·MAIN
CORNICE

DETAIL·CORNICE
OF·FRONT DOORWAY·

·FRONT·ELEVATION·

Shingle roof

Shingle roof

Standing seam Tin roof

PLOT ~ PLAN

2nd floor ceiling

2nd floor Line
1st floor ceiling

Stone band →

Molded brick

First floor Line

Meas. drawn. Kenneth Clark. 1926

COURT·HOUSE·MT·HOLLY·N·J·
FRONT·ELEVATION·AND·VARIOUS·DETAILS

Detail of Front Entrance Doorway

Detail of Stairway

WOOD CORNICE

STONE

WOOD MUNTINS

GLASS

℄ OF BUILDING

WOOD DOORWAY ETC.

WOOD SILL

2 MOLDED BRICK

STONE STEPS

MEAS⁺DRAWN Kenneth Clark 1926

℄ GRADE LINE

COURT · HOUSE · MT · HOLLY · N J

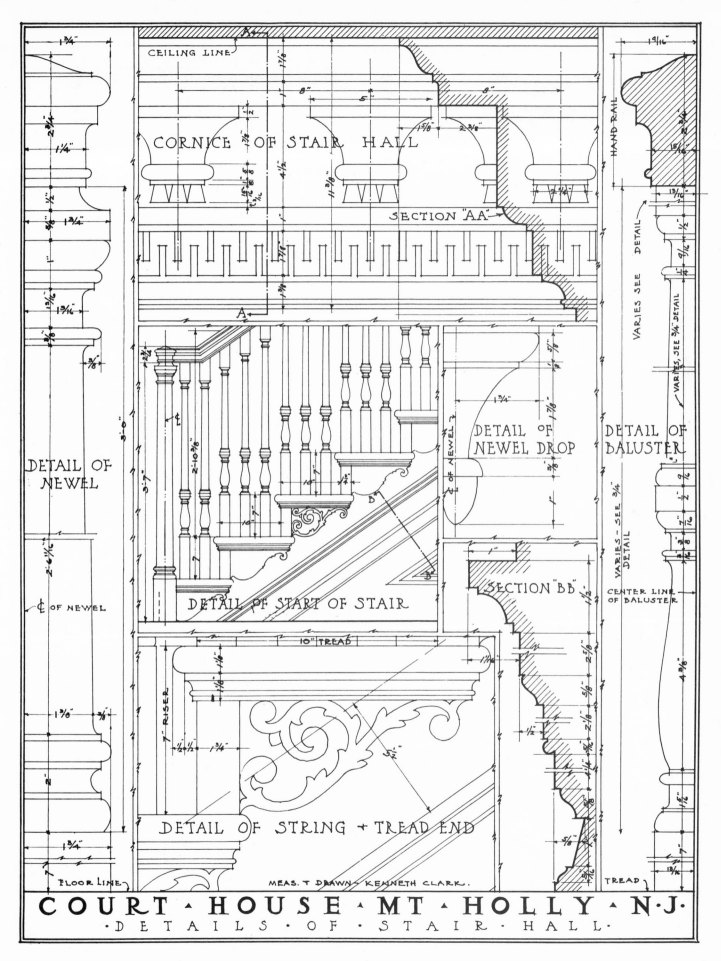

CORNICE OF STAIR HALL

CEILING LINE

SECTION "AA"

DETAIL OF NEWEL

C OF NEWEL

FLOOR LINE

DETAIL OF START OF STAIR

DETAIL OF STRING + TREAD END

10" TREAD

7" RISER

DETAIL OF NEWEL DROP

C OF NEWEL

SECTION "BB"

DETAIL OF BALUSTER

HAND RAIL

VARIES SEE DETAIL

VARIES, SEE 3/4 DETAIL

VARIES - SEE 3/4 DETAIL

CENTER LINE OF BALUSTER

TREAD

MEAS. T DRAWN KENNETH CLARK.

COURT · HOUSE · MT · HOLLY · N·J·
· D E T A I L S · O F · S T A I R · H A L L ·

DETAIL OF RIVER ENTRANCE, "BEVERLY" ON THE POCOMOKE RIVER, MARYLAND.

The ironwork was brought from England about 1775.   The arched
device for carrying the lantern ring over the steps is very unusual.

Eastern Shores of Maryland

Numerous volumes have been published, illustrating the larger and more important works of the "Colonial Period," but with the simpler structures, so logical and full of refinement, we are not so familiar; and yet these simpler buildings are perhaps the best evidence we have of how innate and unaffected was the art of proper building among the early colonists.

It requires no very unusual mind to compile in a fairly satisfactory manner a structure composed of odds and ends selected from that vast storehouse of accumulated "Architectural Styles," even if the fragments are used in a manner never intended by the brain that originally conceived it; but to create from very crude material, without the use of ornament and very often of mouldings, buildings that command our admiration today, bespeaks a natural and unstilted art that was popular and entirely devoid of affectation.

Victor Hugo in his "Notre Dame" states that Architecture lost its function as recorder of human history in the 15th century when Gutenberg invented the printing-press. This seems like a very abstract hypothesis and is perhaps somewhat abstruse, but his argument that before the art of printing was perfected men expressed their highest aspirations in building forms is quite sound. That architecture is crystallized history, or, as Viollet le Duc has said, "Art is the measure of civilization," is only another way of stating Hugo's eloquent argument.

Just why architecture in America deteriorated so woefully in the middle of the 19th century it is difficult to say, but this deterioration is itself a record of a marked change in the intellectual development of a people. In the evolution of our national life, we have reached the era where the striving for ultimate efficiency (some call it Kultur) has eliminated the art sense as a popular movement and has substituted as a lure commercial enterprise. Centering about our cities are great whirlpools of humanity that draw upon the countryside until it is barren of all but the indigent and young, and a few, very few, of those who still have visions of a golden age and dreams of a higher provincialism. There are, however, beyond the whirlpools, quiet eddies not affected by the great commotion, which although they do not gather the flotsam and jetsam of the sea, nevertheless retain that which was committed to their care in perfect contentment.

Those who have succumbed to the lure of the road feel instinctively the witchery of such environment: the long lane of spreading trees arching overhead like the vaulting in some ancient nave, with the sun-flecked roadway running between, where you raise your foot

"BEVERLY" ON THE POCOMOKE RIVER, MARYLAND.   Detail of Porch.

The curious treatment of the transom above the door occurs on both entrances.

from the accelerator and permit the pulse of the motor to beat normally again; the neat whitewashed houses behind green foliage, and the kindly, slow-moving people who always seem to have so much time at their disposal.

It was in such an atmosphere as this that we found ourselves when, at the

COCKRAN'S GRANGE, NEAR MIDDLETOWN, MARYLAND.

instigation of the Editor, we made the long delayed motor trip through Maryland in quest of the Colonial.

Founded in 1632 by Lord Baltimore, Maryland in many ways exhibits in its architecture the tendencies of the Cavalier stock that came with him to America to escape persecution abroad. There is no feeling of arrogance or ostentation about the work, in fact, rather a refinement that.denotes gentility ; but, lacking the spirit of thrift possessed by the Puritans, their houses possess a spaciousness not usually found in the North. They laid out large plantations, kept many slaves who tilled the fields and

raised the excellent thoroughbred stock ; they entertained lavishly and were often ruined by their excesses, as the records show.

It is not, however, the object of this article to treat of the larger and more familiar houses, but rather of the work done on the fertile peninsula best known to the natives as the Eastern Shore of Maryland. This peninsula, sometimes referred to as the "Land of Evergreens," rich in its agricultural pursuits and ravaged very little by the wars that have raged about it, contains many quaint old towns that possess much of the charm of earlier days and innumerable old farmsteads, many of which are still owned and operated by descendants of the original settlers.

One of the most characteristic of these plantations is Beverly, situated on the Pocomoke River near the northern boundary of Virginia. Although possessing considerable architectural merit, I believe that this building has never

BOURKE HOUSE, NEAR CENTREVILLE, MARYLAND.
Characteristic approach to the Maryland farm-house.

"BEVERLY" ON THE POCOMOKE RIVER, MARYLAND.   Entrance Front.   Built in 1774.

"BEVERLY" ON THE POCOMOKE RIVER, MARYLAND.
The approach to this gateway is about one mile long.

been illustrated in any architectural publication before, although mentioned by several authors. It was a very pleasant surprise to me to come unexpectedly upon so excellent an example. The property has been the seat of the Dennis family of Maryland for over two hundred years. Dannock Dennis received the patent to the original estate, containing over one thousand six hundred acres, from Charles II in 1664, and it has remained the homestead of this family for nine generations.

The first house erected on the plantation was destroyed by fire in the 18th century, the present building being erected in 1774. The old family coach with iron steps, leather springs and seats for lackeys still remains in the carriage-shed, and the old family graveyard with its stone tablets recording the passing of nine generations still nestles among the huge shade trees near the house. A broad avenue about one mile in length, flanked by large red cedars, leads to the old road at the eastern end of the plantation. These long shaded lanes are a very characteristic feature of the landscape in Maryland, even the simplest farms having splendid approaches of this sort, as illustrated in the photographs of Cockran's Grange near Middletown and the Bourke House at Centreville.

In wandering through Maryland one is very much impressed by the beauty of these lanes leading up to the white farm buildings, usually so well grouped and surrounded by orchards and shade trees. The illustration of the farm-house near Chestertown gives some idea of the effect of these interesting white buildings among the trees. This building also conveys some idea of the simplicity of the detail and the excellent massing of these simple farm-houses.

Many of the smaller houses seen along the roadside might well serve as models for the moderate-sized houses that are being erected throughout the country in such atrociously bad taste; in fact, one is strongly impressed by the superiority of the crudest negro quarters in Maryland as compared with the average mechanic's home in more progressive sections. The roofs are always just the right pitch with only cornice enough to perform the proper functions of a cornice, and these with very simple mouldings, if any. The cornice was seldom

OLD HOUSE IN CHESTERTOWN, MARYLAND.

This quaint old town was the original port of entry for Maryland before Baltimore was chosen and contains many excellent houses built during the early part of the 18th century.

OLD SLAVE QUARTERS
ON MARYLAND
STATE ROAD.

FARM-HOUSE NEAR
WESTOWN, MARYLAND

STEPHENS HOUSE,
GALENA, MARYLAND.

OLD HOUSE NEAR
KINGSTON, MARYLAND.

EARLY FARM-HOUSE ON
MARYLAND STATE ROAD.

OLD FARM-HOUSE NEAR
CHESTERTOWN, MARYLAND.

OLD HOUSE NEAR CECILTON, MARYLAND.
Showing characteristic method of enlarging the building from generation to generation.

carried up the gable ends, these being usually finished with a face-board over which the shingles project slightly. The chimneys were always of brick and usually very generous in size. The gambrel roof is seldom seen in this section. In enlarging the houses it was usual to prolong the main axis of the building, producing long, low lines with roofs at different levels. Very often the addition was larger than the original building, as in the old house near Cecilton, above, where we have three distinct divisions, the smaller section being probably the original. Sometimes, however, wings were carried out to the rear, as in the old house near Kingston, below, but the treatment of the intersection of the roofs and grouping of gables was always somewhat similar and forms one of the charms of these simple buildings.

OLD HOUSE NEAR KINGSTON, MARYLAND.
Another example showing interesting development of additions.

The Stephens House at Galena, formerly Georgetown Cross Roads, was originally a log cabin and is reputed to be two hundred years old. As was very often the case where the early settlers became more prosperous and sought more commodious surroundings, the building was extended and the entire construction covered with White Pine siding, and with this protection many excellent examples of the first houses erected in this country have been preserved.

The road running past this building is a portion of the Maryland State Road, which runs the entire length of the Eastern Shore and is one of the most excellent roads imaginable and one that the architectural student might profitably make use of if he would see evidence of the fact that a proper sense of proportion was a common heritage in the early days of our history, and not possessed solely by the designers of the more pretentious Georgian examples.

TWO OLD FARM-HOUSES NEAR POCOMOKE CITY, MARYLAND.
It is interesting to note curious fence-posts which show the English influence.

ENTRANCE DETAIL

THE SAMUEL CHASE HOUSE
COR. MARYLAND AVENUE
& KING GEORGE STREET
ANNAPOLIS, MARYLAND

Annapolis, Maryland

TURNING back in the history of Annapolis to the early period before the great houses were built, we reconstruct a picture which might be entitled—the town with a future. The first settled areas are marked by modest clusters of buildings with wide unoccupied acres between, through which embryonic streets have been cut. The center of the peninsula is high ground upon which the seat of government is established with church adjoining. The principal streets radiate to the waterfront along Spa Creek and the Severn River. On the former lies the large estate of Carrollton and just upstream is Acton, the first land-grant hereabouts. The entire waterfront is reserved for building sites save only for the dock which faces the harbor. In the triangular area based upon the dock and rising to Church Circle lie the shops, storehouses, and smaller dwellings, the latter steep-roofed like plantation houses and varied only occasionally by larger two-storied structures. The Carroll and Tasker estates of Spa Creek are thus cut off by the business of Main Street from the easterly dwelling area along Prince George Street where early settlers like Jennings, Dorsey, and Brewer have established their homes facing toward the river.

Traffic hums about the dock where hogsheads of tobacco rolling in from the counties are jostled by alluring bales of merchandize from over the sea. There is a steady influx of new colonists and it is evident that the older houses resting here so picturesquely amid their foliage are soon to have fine neighbors. When they have all come and their fine houses have been built our pan-orama will turn to another period in which the completed city shows a fascinating picture of Renaissance luxury; in Anapolis it is called "The Golden Age."

So much of the early period is gone that reconstruction is difficult. For example the first governor's mansion built on Cornhill Street for Francis Nicholson (1694-9) has become only a memory, and the first church, the first state house, the first armory are known only by fragmentary descriptions. The architecture of the mid-Eighteenth Century has been more fortunate. Beginning with Governor Ogle, who came out in 1732 and served intermittently over a period of twenty years, the proprietary governors took a leading part in the development of architecture. Governor Ogle's house, built about 1742, stands today as evidence of his good taste in building. His son inherited the house and made various additions, one of which may have been the octagonal wing at the rear.

One is led to believe that Governor Ogle also built the splendid country mansion of Belair in Prince George's County and certainly in his time the first part of the Carroll house (1735) was built, as well as the Brice house (1740), and the Bordley and the Jennings houses.

The Carroll house represents more than one period of colonial building but the additions were ever in keeping with the original so that it presents today a unified picture of large and lordly mansion. True, the plan lacks dignity because of the crowded stair hall and narrowed circulations; yet, its lofty mass and good brickwork show how a fine building may be accomplished by simple

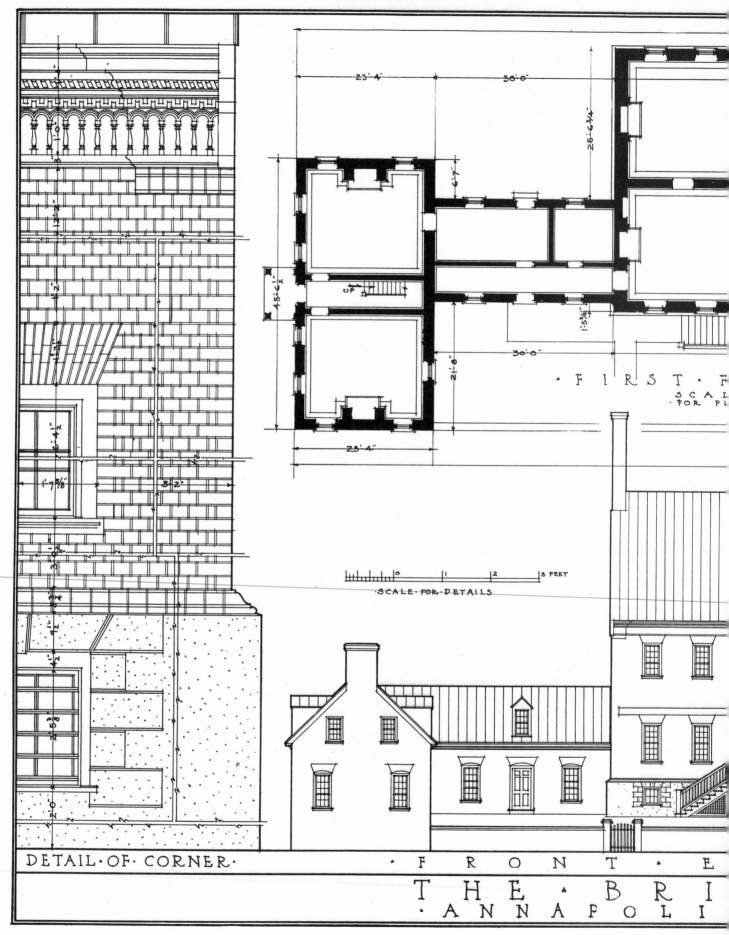

DETAIL·OF·CORNER·

·F R O N T · E

T H E · B R I

· A N N A P O L I

Drawings are repro

Dimensions visible on drawing:
23'·4"
30'·0"
25'·6¾"
6'·7"
45'·6½"
1'·5¾"
21'·8"
30'·0"
23'·4"
UP

·F I R S T · F
SCAL
·FOR·PL

SCALE·FOR·DETAILS
0   1   2   3 FEET

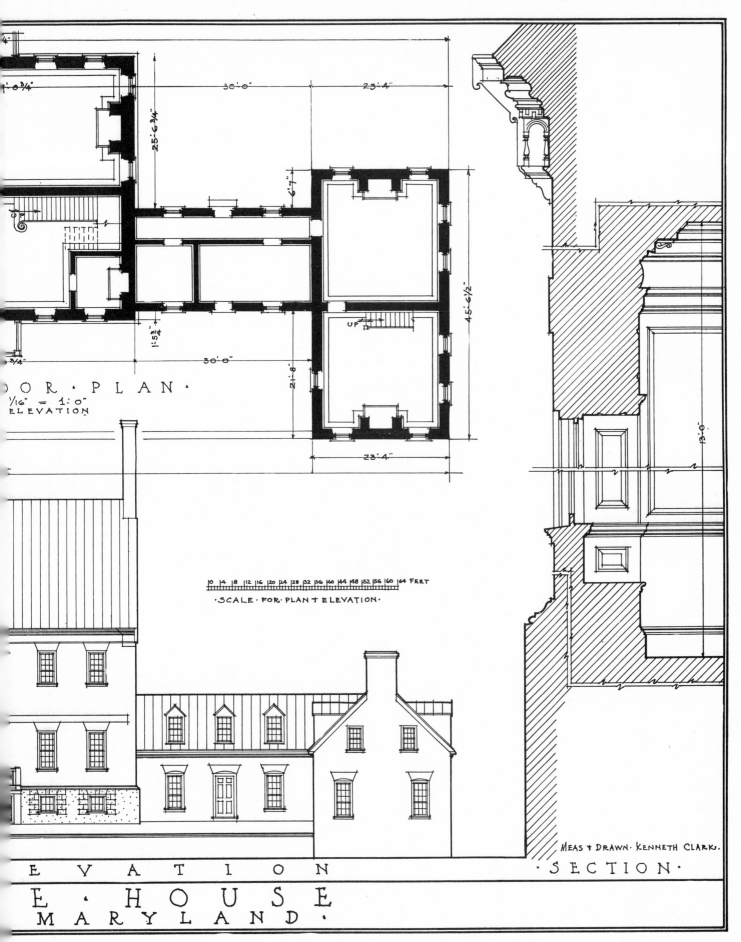

30'-0" 23'-4"

25'-6¾"

6'-7"

45'-6½"

1'-5¾"

30'-0"

21'-8"

23'-4"

OOR · PLAN ·
⅛₆" = 1'-0"
ELEVATION

13'-0"

10 14 18 12 16 20 24 28 32 36 40 44 48 52 56 60 64 FEET

· SCALE · FOR · PLAN ↑ ELEVATION ·

MEAS ↑ DRAWN · KENNETH CLARK ·

EVATION   · SECTION ·

E · HOUSE
MARYLAND ·

ctly at scale marked

The BRICE HOUSE, *Built in* 1740

Corner East and Prince George Streets
ANNAPOLIS, MARYLAND

MEASURED DRAWINGS *from*
The George F. Lindsay Collection

FRONT ELEVATION

A BEAUTIFUL GEORGIAN STAIRWAY IN THE
BRICE HOUSE, ANNAPOLIS, MARYLAND

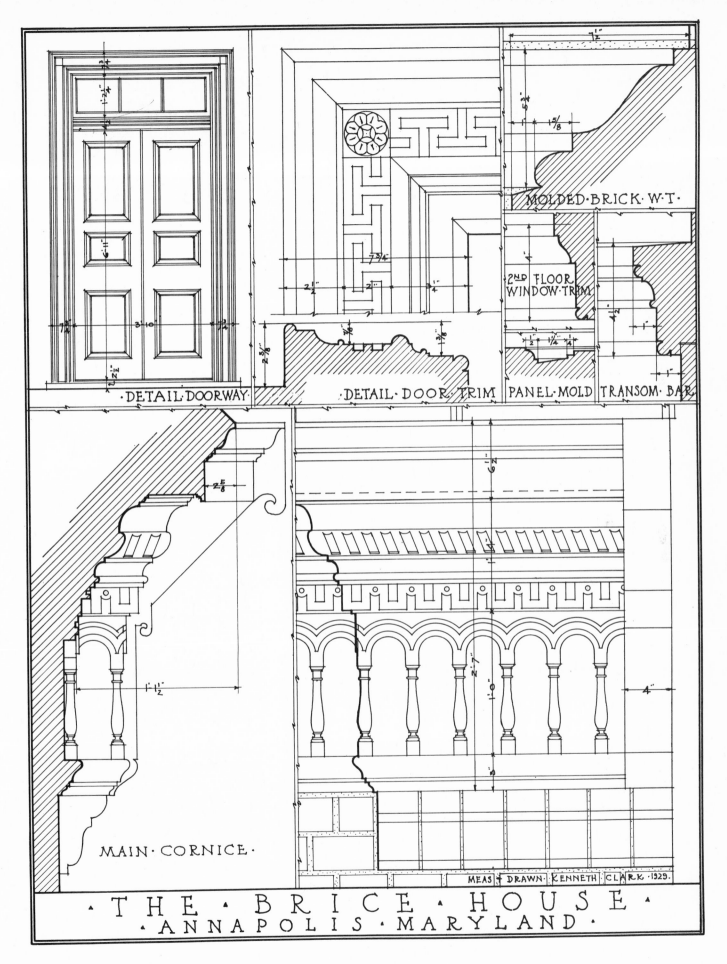

· DETAIL · DOORWAY ·

· DETAIL · DOOR · TRIM ·

PANEL · MOLD

TRANSOM · BAR

MOLDED · BRICK · W.T.

· 2ND · FLOOR · WINDOW · TRIM ·

· MAIN · CORNICE ·

MEAS + DRAWN · KENNETH · CLARK · 1929·

· T H E · B R I C E · H O U S E ·
· A N N A P O L I S · M A R Y L A N D ·

131

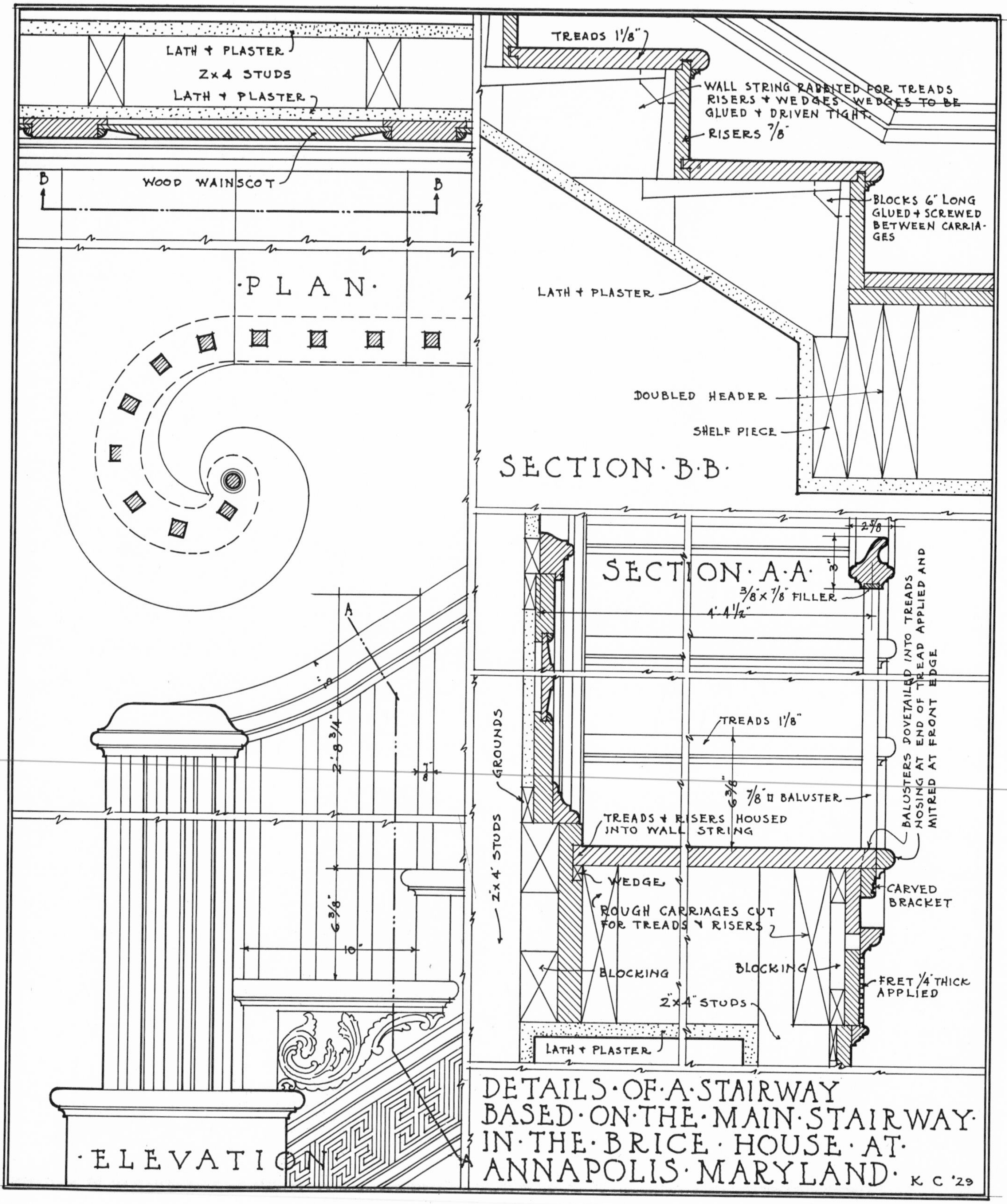
LATH + PLASTER
2×4 STUDS
LATH + PLASTER
WOOD WAINSCOT
B
B
·PLAN·
TREADS 1 1/8"
WALL STRING RABBITED FOR TREADS RISERS + WEDGES. WEDGES TO BE GLUED + DRIVEN TIGHT.
RISERS 7/8"
BLOCKS 6" LONG GLUED + SCREWED BETWEEN CARRIAGES
LATH + PLASTER
DOUBLED HEADER
SHELF PIECE
SECTION·B·B·
SECTION·A·A·
2 1/8
3"
3/8 × 7/8" FILLER
4'-4 1/2"
TREADS 1 1/8"
GROUNDS
6 3/8"
7/8" □ BALUSTER
BALUSTERS DOVETAILED INTO TREADS NOSING AT END OF TREAD APPLIED AND MITRED AT FRONT EDGE
TREADS + RISERS HOUSED INTO WALL STRING
2"×4" STUDS
WEDGE
ROUGH CARRIAGES CUT FOR TREADS + RISERS
CARVED BRACKET
BLOCKING
BLOCKING
FRET 1/4" THICK APPLIED
2"×4" STUDS
LATH + PLASTER
A
2'-8 3/4"
6 3/8"
10"
A
·ELEVATION·
DETAILS·OF·A·STAIRWAY BASED·ON·THE·MAIN·STAIRWAY· IN·THE·BRICE·HOUSE·AT· ANNAPOLIS·MARYLAND·
K C '29

THE CARROLL
HOUSE,
SPA CREEK,
ANNAPOLIS,
MARYLAND

THE WILLIAM
PACA HOUSE,
PRINCE
GEORGE
STREET,
ANNAPOLIS,
MARYLAND

133

DETAIL OF DOORWAY IN
OCTAGONAL WING AT THE REAR

THE OGLE HOUSE, 33 COLLEGE
AVENUE, ANNAPOLIS, MARYLAND

Residence of Governor Samuel Ogle 1747-1752

means. The segmental arches are among the few in Annapolis.

The Brice house is like Carrollton in that it faces south; generally the houses are turned obliquely to the principal points of the compass with the result that every side gets the sun. Back of the Brice house and probably over twenty years later than it in date of erection is the Paca house, the home of William Paca, a Signer of the Declaration of Independence.

Returning to governors and governors' mansions, we discover that McDowell Hall, the present main building of St. John's College, was originally erected as "Government House" during the term of Thomas Bladen, governor from 1742 to 1747. The site selected was on the open ground toward Dorsey's Creek north of the State House which had been built about the year 1700 with W. Bladen as architect. Construction on the new government house started in 1745 but the governor had conceived it on so expensive a scale that the House of Burgesses objected to the cost and finally refused further appropriations. At this point, it is said, the walls were up and the rafters in place; but work was stopped perforce for lack of funds and thus the building stood a skeleton open to the winds for forty years. The dream of Duff, the architect, who is said to have brought out the plans with him from Scotland, remained unrealized until another architect, probably Robert Key, finished the building for the uses of St. John's College. And thus, with the addition of a later cupola, it stands today: dour, Caledonian, and uncompromising—as was doubtless the governor in his dealings with the burgesses.

With this exception however architectural projects were fostered in a harmonious atmosphere. In the case of Governor Sharpe and the people we find only considerateness on the one hand and unbounded popularity on the other. As between the earlier and the later work a difference must be kept in mind, namely, that the earlier was more individual and in a sense experimental while the later work held close to an accepted style, established in days of opulence when society realized itself. English architecture was the vogue while English political loyalties were fading; but the personality of Governor Sharpe was such as to pacify the political belligerents throughout the province. Long before the Stamp Act battle of 1765 which took place within sight of his Annapolis mansion he might have known that the American temper was tending toward revolution and yet his patronage was lent to the peaceful development of a loyal colony and his friends were the builders of the period.

John Ridout was secretary to the governor and came out with him in 1753. Seven years later at the age of twenty-eight he completed the house which stands to-day beautifully preserved on Duke of Gloucester Street facing the old mansion of Carrollton. Some of the best elements of the mature period are realized in its design, faintly reminiscent of their remote progenitors of the English manor house. The wings are rather detached in composition and projecting to the front. The refined windows, the scholarly doorway, and the plain brick belt course are features in a memorable façade the effect of which is heightened by the delicate pattern of the "all header" bond, peculiar to Annapolis but used first about 1650 in Governor Calvert's country house, Mount Airy, in Prince George's County. In plan the Ridout house is like the Brice and Randall houses in that the front door is not on center of the hall. On either hand is a fine room, with stair seen through a graceful archway. At the rear are drawing and dining rooms overlooking the terraced garden from which we are privileged to see the intimate side of the house.

Less fortunate in preservation is the house of Dr. Upton Scott, another contemporary of Governor Sharpe. It stands back from Shipwright Street facing Spa Creek and lacks the wings with which most of the local mansions were provided. Its age is probably little less than that of the Ridout house but, failing the care which that family has ever given to its ancestral home, the Scott house has lost much in quality. One prefers to think of it as shown in old pictures taken before it was shuttered and painted and before its long garden wall was removed. The singular simplicity of the plan awakes a suspicion that the designer was actuated by the practical needs of a physician's house rather than by the more intangible values of architecture.

Governor Eden who held office from 1769 until the war, lived for a time at the Scott house, and it may be that he entertained his friend, George Washington, here. At all events he was patron and friend of the architect, Robert Key, and generally exercised a friendly influence

LOOKING TOWARD STATE HOUSE CIRCLE, ANNAPOLIS, MARYLAND

THE MARYLAND STATE HOUSE — BUILT 1772

on architecture even when the colonists were turning toward independence.

The Chase house motives are as well known as any in Annapolis. It is lofty and manorial: the English manor house in type but built by an American patriot. The plan shows that wings were originally intended; but they were never built. In view of this fact we find the conception of the façade to be nearly identical with Winslow Hall in Buckinghamshire, England, which was erected about the year 1700. The coincidence is but one of many which might be traced. In each case of similarity we find that the American building followed but slowly the English original with an interval of two or three generations between. In plan also, but with smaller dimensions, the Chase house follows the precedent of Renaissance manor houses in the mother country. It is unique in Annapolis but unfortunately without garden setting; would that it might have been built in the earlier day when so many Annapolis acres were undeveloped, when it was only "a town with a future."

By the time the war began, Governor Eden was forced to leave and the period was completed—the future realized. Fortunately for us the city has lain ever since in the amber of inspiring precedent and graceful memory. In the search for American backgrounds it furnishes a field that appeals no less to the reason than to the sentiment. Peculiarly rich in the charm of colonial settlement, it furnishes a living memorial of things that are human and universal—the substance from which architecture is made.

GARDEN ELEVATION

THE DR. UPTON SCOTT HOUSE, SHIPWRIGHT STREET, ANNAPOLIS, MARYLAND

DETAIL OF ENTRANCE DOORWAY

THE DR. UPTON SCOTT HOUSE, SHIPWRIGHT STREET, ANNAPOLIS, MARYLAND

DETAIL OF HALL
THE DR. UPTON SCOTT HOUSE, SHIPWRIGHT STREET, ANNAPOLIS, MARYLAND

McDOWELL HALL, ST. JOHN'S COLLEGE, ANNAPOLIS, MARYLAND

Thos. Bladen, Fifth Royal Governor of Maryland began this building in 1745 for a Governor's palace.
It stood unfinished for many years.

THE JOHN RIDOUT HOUSE,
ANNAPOLIS, MARYLAND

DETAIL OF MAIN FACADE
AND FLANKING WING

DETAIL OF GARDEN ENTRANCE

THE JOHN RIDOUT HOUSE,
GARDEN ELEVATION,
ANNAPOLIS, MARYLAND

WEST DOORWAY

WEST ELEVATION—MAIN HOUSE

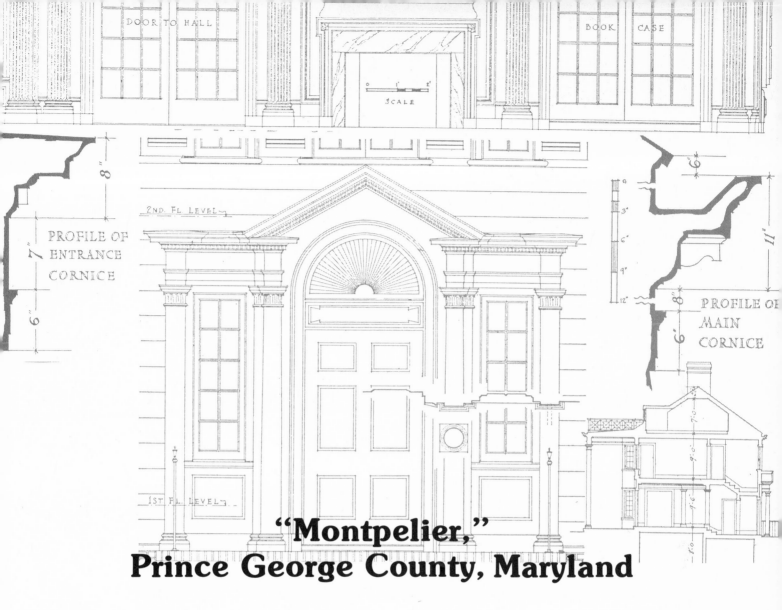

"Montpelier,"
Prince George County, Maryland

THE Snowden-Long House, or as it is more familiarly known to its neighbors, "Montpelier," lies off the beaten track of tourist travel. Though it is one of the masterpieces of architecture, of its period and locality, it is little known outside the circle of a chosen few who have been fortunate enough to see the house.

About two miles off the main Baltimore-Washington turnpike, on a gravel road connecting Laurel and Bowie, Prince George County, Maryland, "Montpelier" stands on the summit of a considerable hill, surrounded by trees that almost hide it from sight. Its setting is ideal. Expansive views extend in every direction over broad acres that once heard the crooning chants of the negro slaves, at their tasks, who made possible such estates in the days when Wall Street was just a street and supporting revenues were tilled and dug from the earth with sweaty toil. It stands there today, practically unchanged except for the minor alterations necessary to make it habitable in this day and age, a monument of simple grace and sturdy strength to the skill and artistry of those who built it.

Based on the same general design and plan as other Maryland houses—the Brice and the Hammond Houses of Annapolis and "Whitehall," once the home of Horatio Sharp, an early Governor of Maryland—"Montpelier" is individual in many respects. The interiors, particularly, have a charm of intimacy and scale that may be equaled by others but not surpassed.

The definite date of its erection is not known at any source available to the author, but it is recorded that Thomas Snowden was born here in 1751 and that the house was built by his father. Montpelier was known as the "old Nicholas Snowden place" to the historians of the Chesapeake Bay country. Snowden, senior, was a man of quiet, sober tastes, whose individuality was expressed in the simple exterior, devoid of useless ornament, but dignified and rather austere.

Young Thomas Snowden, is credited with adding the wings to the main house and the interior decorations which make this house so outstanding. In fact, there

EAST ELEVATION OF NORTH WING

EAST ELEVATION

is a tradition to the effect that he, personally, carved the ornament in the Southeast drawing room.

That the Snowdens were Quakers, and wealthy, is attested by the record that Thomas Snowden was forbidden by the fellow members of his Quaker church to come to meeting because of his great wealth and possessions. To placate them and to show that his heart was touched with the true Christian spirit, he liberated one hundred of his slaves as a peace offering and was reinstated in the good graces of his pious and perhaps envious brethren.

The grounds of "Montpelier" include a wonderful box garden, the number and size of whose plants is amazing. An axis at right angles to the box lined walk leading to the front door runs one hundred and forty feet parallel to the front of the house through hedges forming a miniature *pleache allée* to a garden house of wood that is quaint in design but somehow "just right."

The exterior of "Montpelier" presents two almost identical elevations, facing East and West, the only difference between them being the angular plan of the wings on the East front and a more elaborate detail treatment of that doorway. The brickwork is laid in Flemish Bond and is rich in color, the joints, one quarter inch wide of white mortar having the familiar trowel struck line that is used in the walls of the Hammond House.

The roofs, originally of shingle, have been slated and shutters have been added, which is an unusual feature of houses in this part of the country where inside blinds seem to be in universal use. The cornice, executed in wood, is detailed conventionally, but is well proportioned as a crowning member of the facade.

The window lintels are of ground brick with the mortar joints narrowed so as to be almost imperceptible.

A moulded brick water table is used in the main house and wings, but the level is not carried through, the wing base being below that of the main house.

The plan of the main house conforms in many respects to the usual Maryland *partie*, but it varies from its prototypes in having a wide hall running through the main house from front to back that gives a fine feeling of spaciousness. The vista through the front door is charm-

WEST ELEVATION—GENERAL DETAIL

EAST DOORWAY

GARDEN HOUSE

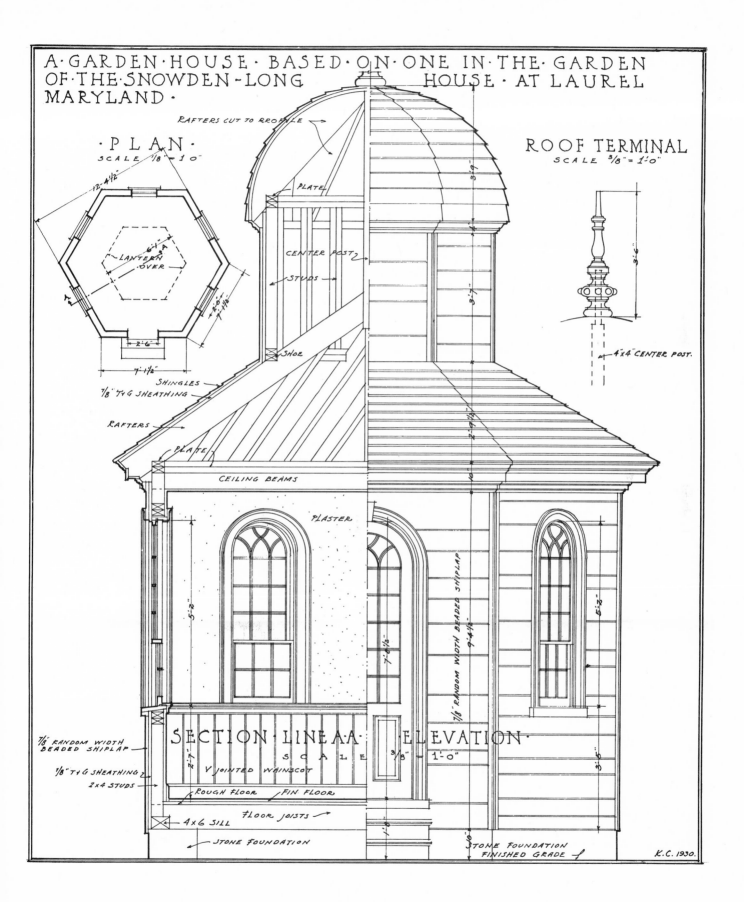

A·GARDEN·HOUSE·BASED·ON·ONE IN·THE·GARDEN
OF·THE·SNOWDEN~LONG   HOUSE·AT·LAUREL
MARYLAND·

RAFTERS CUT TO RROFILE

·PLAN·
SCALE ⅛" = 1'0"

12-4½

LANTERN OVER

6'-1"

2'-0"
7'-1½"

2'-6"

7'-1½"

ROOF TERMINAL
SCALE ⅜" = 1'-0"

PLATE

CENTER POST

STUDS

SHOE

4x4 CENTER POST.

SHINGLES

⅞" T&G SHEATHING

RAFTERS

PLATE

CEILING BEAMS

PLASTER

⅞" RANDOM WIDTH BEADED SHIPLAP

SECTION·LINE·A·A·   ·ELEVATION·
SCALE ⅜" = 1'-0"

⅞" RANDOM WIDTH
BEADED SHIPLAP

⅞" T&G SHEATHING

2x4 STUDS

V JOINTED WAINSCOT

ROUGH FLOOR   FIN FLOOR

FLOOR JOISTS

4x6 SILL

STONE FOUNDATION

STONE FOUNDATION
FINISHED GRADE

K.C. 1930.

147

ing. The great hedges of box form the foreground to a landscape of interest and beauty with trees, whether intentionally placed or not, coming at just the right spots to frame and finish the picture.

A well executed plaster entablature adorns the hall; its freize is ornamented with symbolic decorations of wreaths of wheat surrounding a scythe, a rake and an arrow, alternating with a fruit filled vase and the whole joined by a vine-like plant with graceful scrolls and flowers. A similar freize and cornice, though slightly varying in detail, is used around the second floor stair hall.

The staircase has been designed and placed so that, while it forms an important part of the hall as a whole, it does not obstruct the view, since the hall is widened to receive it. It is a broad, inviting flight, facing on the second floor a wide eliptical arched opening. The details and balusters are simple in design and a wainscot continues up the stairs and around the second floor hall.

DETAIL OF ENTABLATURE

HALL—THE SNOWDEN-LONG HOUSE

The feature room of the house, now known as the southeast drawing room, is an example of the design and execution of the period that is an inspiration and causes those with appreciative eyes to bless and revere the artistic sense and the superior craftsmanship of its creators. The design is not "book" architecture and though the eggs and darts, lambs tongues and all the other conventional elements are here it does not conform to the usual standards of design.

There is no symmetrical wall in this room, except the south wall; no axes are acknowledged by mantel, doors, or windows; yet it has a feeling of symmetry and spacing that is most satisfactory.

The workmanship is remarkable. Mantel, trim, wainscot, china-closet and cornice are all of carved wood and all are superbly executed. The whole room has been painted a lovely shade of blue which adds charm and a livable quality to the ensemble.

The Northeast and Southwest rooms on the first floor are much more simply treated with an unusually large mantel in the former and a wood paneled mantel wall in the latter.

An item of interest in the Southeast and Northeast rooms is that the doors on the mantel walls are only 6'-1" high, while those leading into the hall are 6'8¾". Why this was done is not entirely clear, but perhaps it seemed to the designer that it added scale and importance to the mantels. We moderns with our passion for "lining up" things have missed a few tricks by so doing and have sacrificed the very charm that these rooms possess in the quest of perfect symmetry and axial lines which look so well in plan but, as is here proved, do not count so much in actual execution.

The second floor rooms are not elaborate though each contains a well designed mantel. Really unique is the one in the northeast chamber with its broken pediment over the mantel. The coat of arms in the broken pediment is that of the present owner, but evidence was found on the wall that furnished precedent for this type of ornament.

"Montpelier" has been fortunate, beyond its peers, in finally falling into the hands of owners who appreciate and cherish its beauties. It has been restored sympathetically and made habitable with no apparent marring and it has been furnished throughout with a taste and discernment that make it a wonderful example of what the Colonial gentleman of the eighteenth century considered a becoming dwelling place.

SOUTHEAST DRAWING ROOM
THE SNOWDEN·LONG HOUSE
LAUREL, MARYLAND

MEASURED DRAWINGS *from*
The George F. Lindsay Collection

CORNER OF SOUTHEAST DRAWING ROOM—FORMERLY THE DINING ROOM

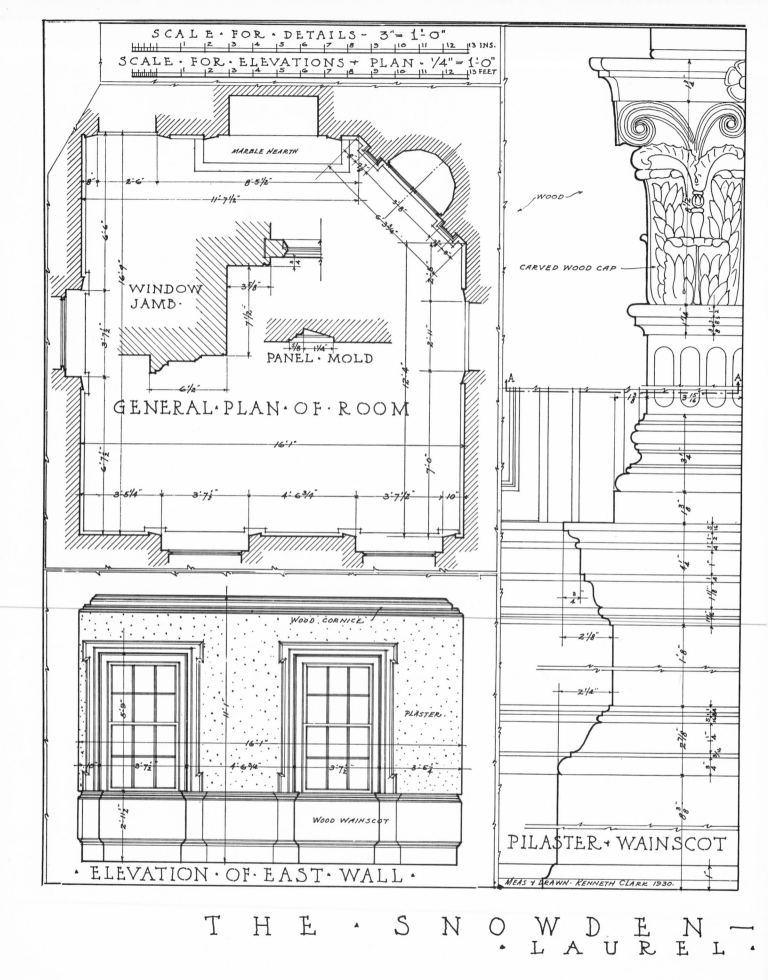

SCALE · FOR · DETAILS · 3" = 1'-0"

SCALE · FOR · ELEVATIONS + PLAN · ¼" = 1'-0"

MARBLE HEARTH

WINDOW
JAMB·

PANEL · MOLD

GENERAL · PLAN · OF · ROOM

WOOD

CARVED WOOD CAP

· ELEVATION · OF · EAST · WALL ·

WOOD CORNICE

PLASTER·

WOOD WAINSCOT

PILASTER + WAINSCOT

MEAS + DRAWN · KENNETH CLARK · 1930.

T H E · S N O W D E N —
· L A U R E L ·

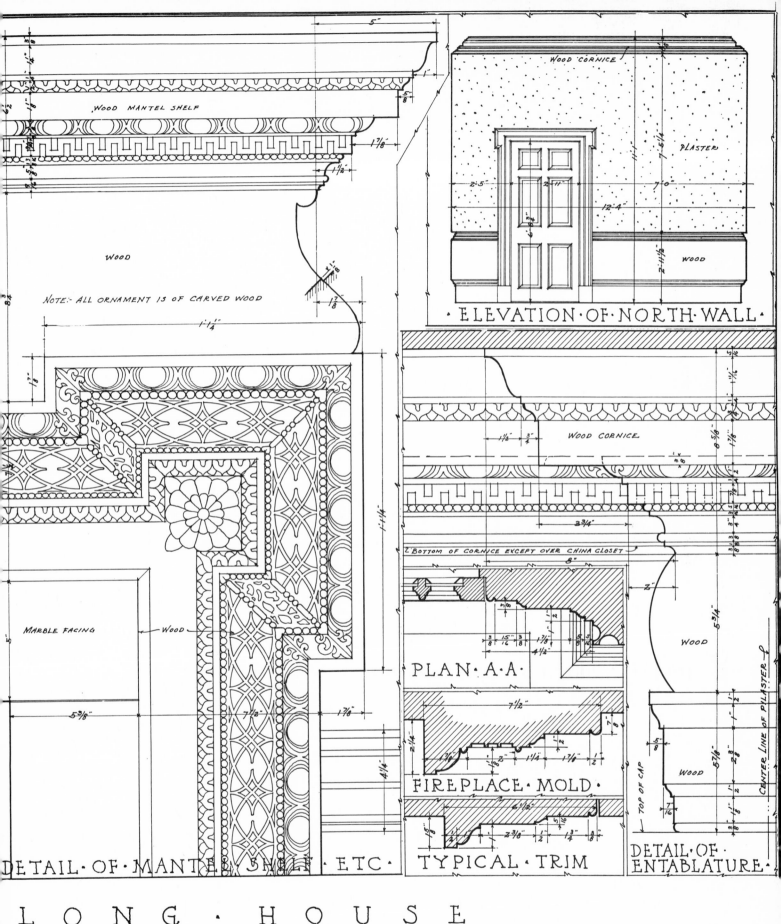

WOOD MANTEL SHELF

WOOD

NOTE:- ALL ORNAMENT IS OF CARVED WOOD

MARBLE FACING   WOOD

ELEVATION·OF·NORTH·WALL·

PLASTER

WOOD

WOOD CORNICE

WOOD CORNICE

Bottom of cornice except over china closet

PLAN·A·A·

FIREPLACE·MOLD·

WOOD

WOOD

DETAIL·OF·MANTEL·SHELF·ETC·   TYPICAL·TRIM   DETAIL·OF·ENTABLATURE·

L O N G · H O U S E
M A R Y L A N D ·

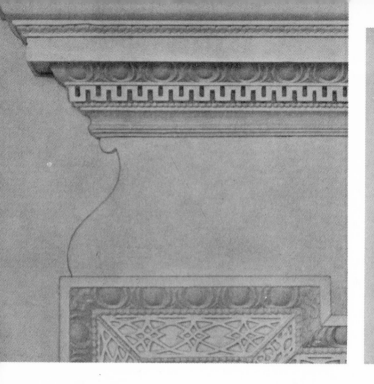

DETAIL OF MANTEL

MANTEL WALL

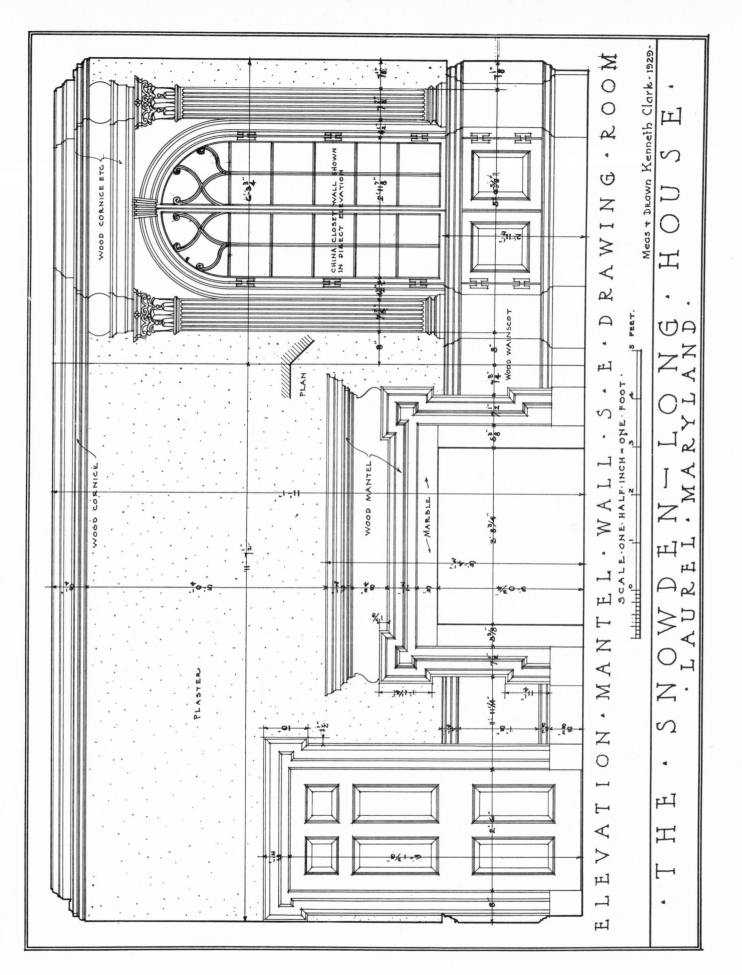

ELEVATION · MANTEL · WALL · S.E · DRAWING · ROOM

Meas + Drawn Kenneth Clark · 1929 ·

SCALE · ONE · HALF · INCH = ONE · FOOT

5 FEET.

· THE · SNOWDEN–LONG · HOUSE ·
· LAUREL · MARYLAND ·

WOOD CORNICE ETC

WOOD CORNICE

PLASTER

CHINA CLOSET WALL SHOWN
IN DIRECT ELEVATION

PLAN

WOOD MANTEL

MARBLE

WOOD WAINSCOT

NORTHEAST ROOM—FIRST FLOOR

MANTEL, NORTHEAST BED ROOM

SOUTHWEST ROOM
—FIRST FLOOR

FIRST FLOOR HALL

HALL, SECOND FLOOR

STAIRWAY DETAIL

THE JONES–SAPPINGTON HOUSE, LIBERTYTOWN, FREDERICK COUNTY, MARYLAND

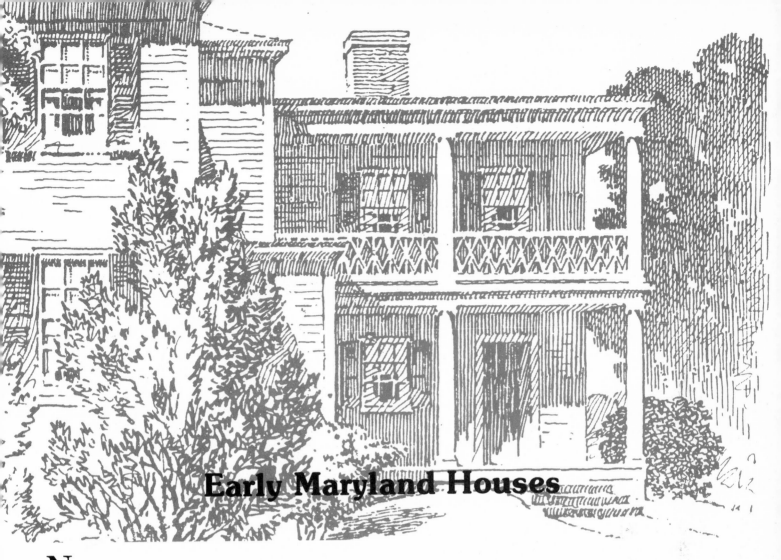

Early Maryland Houses

NO WHERE is the spirit of our Colonial past better preserved than in the Tidewater country of Maryland and Virginia. A good life was lived and traditions of urbanity and hospitality wove themselves in the fabric of its buildings. Time has dealt gently with this district and apart from a mellowness that comes with age there has been no great change with the passing of several centuries. There is still a gracious spirit hovering over the broad waters of the Chesapeake and its estuaries and many a scene does not vary the least from the same scene when the fine brick residence whose gardens sloped in lovely terraces down to the river's edge was new and a bustling centre of prosperous enterprise. The prosperity has gone, it is true, but in its place is a simple dignity and brooding retrospect.

What constitutes the charm of our old buildings it is not difficult to say. First comes simplicity. Almost all our early houses are simple, even the finest are little more than glorified farmhouses and each and every house is eloquent of the kind of life it houses,—which is fitness or appropriateness. The materials are native, well understood, which means honesty and a certain frank courage. A sense of site contributes, for it is rare that the physical features of the landscape are not incorporated, and garden features often extend widely, achiev-

ing a happy marriage of house to land which in Architecture is very near to contentment.

The traditions the early settlers to Maryland brought with them from England, the climate, and the ways of Colonial life all conspired to the ends we illustrate. The settler frequently lived the life of a landed proprietor in almost feudal conditions of authority. Land was abundant and he nearly always, unlike his contemporary in New England, built in the country, away from towns. The natural functions of his household determined the plan of his house. The large central house was designed for his immediate household. Servants were plentiful and undoubtedly gay, and noisy, after their kind. What more fitting than that they and their duties be somewhat away from the family, housed in a wing. The Maryland settler was familiar, by formal education, with the classics and liked symmetry and balance. A wing corresponding to the service quarters balanced the composition and accommodated the business of the proprietor and often a school. Here he met his steward, and his dependents' children received their education. In Virginia these three departments of the household were usually housed in three independent buildings. In Maryland the climate made it convenient to connect the three elements of the architectural composition with

159

DOORWAY, THE JONES-SAPPINGTON HOUSE

160

covered passage ways. And this is the Genesis of the typical Maryland Colonial plan—her first contribution to Colonial Architecture.

The Brice House in Annapolis illustrates this composite plan. It is situated on a street so narrow it is impossible to appreciate the mass which is its most distinguished feature. Few can realize that the height of the building from the eaves to the ridge of the roof is almost as great as the height from the eaves to the first floor line. With its great central house and the two wings much lower, set at right angles, and connected by low covered passages, it is the finest expression of the distinctive Maryland plan. The façade of the main house is laid entirely in headers and not the usual Flemish bond seen in the wings. The writer ventures the criticism that the Palladian window in the second story is needlessly complicated and too crowded and, with its relieving arch cut by the cornice, is poorly composed. But withal, with its great height, beautiful fenistration and towering gable chimneys it remains one of the most effective of all Colonial houses,—a monument to some past designer of more than average taste and imagination.

The interior details are especially good. The wall panels and cornices are of plaster, the trims, chair rails and mantels of wood with carved ornamentation. The mantel brackets show most spirited carving but unfortunately the fire openings have been filled in inside the original marble facing with recent brick work. The modillioned cornice suggests an origin in the ornamental

HOUSE, NEAR CHESTERTOWN, KENT COUNTY, MARYLAND

interiors of the Palazzo Massimi.

Although the first settlement in Maryland was on the penninsula between the Potomac River and the Chesapeake Bay in what is now St. Mary's County, the settlements very early spread out to the north following the rivers and Bay. Calvert County, the penninsula between the Patuxent River and the Bay, was settled only a few years later. Then followed in quick succession Prince George, Anne Arundel and Charles County, all south of Baltimore. Throughout this period the waterways were the highways and practically all of the important houses were located in direct reference to the water.

An exception to this rule is the house near upper Marlboro in Prince George County, built by the Calvert Family—the Lords Proprietors of the Colony; as a Hunting Lodge. It is variously known as Mt. Airy or The Dower House. The original house is quite small and although it lacks the advantages of a water view, it has the favorite terraces sloping rather suddenly to the farm lands beyond. It is a simple one story brick structure with a second story in a gambrel roof. The central and taller portion is flanked by two lower wings. The façade of the main building like the Brice House is built entirely of headers. There is the local tradition that the design is one of the first ever made by Christopher Wrenn, when he was a boy but 14 years old. It is said he was recommended to Lord Baltimore on one of Baltimore's visits to London andwas given by him the problem of designing for him, on his estate in Maryland, a hunting lodge. In proof of the tradition one's attention is called to the varying size of all doors and windows, but one fails to see why this should be attributed to inexperienced genius rather than inexperienced workmen or even time itself. The building is now much larger than the original Hunting Lodge, although almost all of very early origin, but unfortunately suffers greatly from neglect and a far from discriminating and wise restoration. The old place, one of the houses of the First of Maryland Colonial Fami-

PANELING, STAIRCASE, CUPBOARD AND MANTELPIECE FROM A MARYLAND HOME BUILT ABOUT 1690
Now installed at the Baltimore Art Museum. See construction details on facing page.

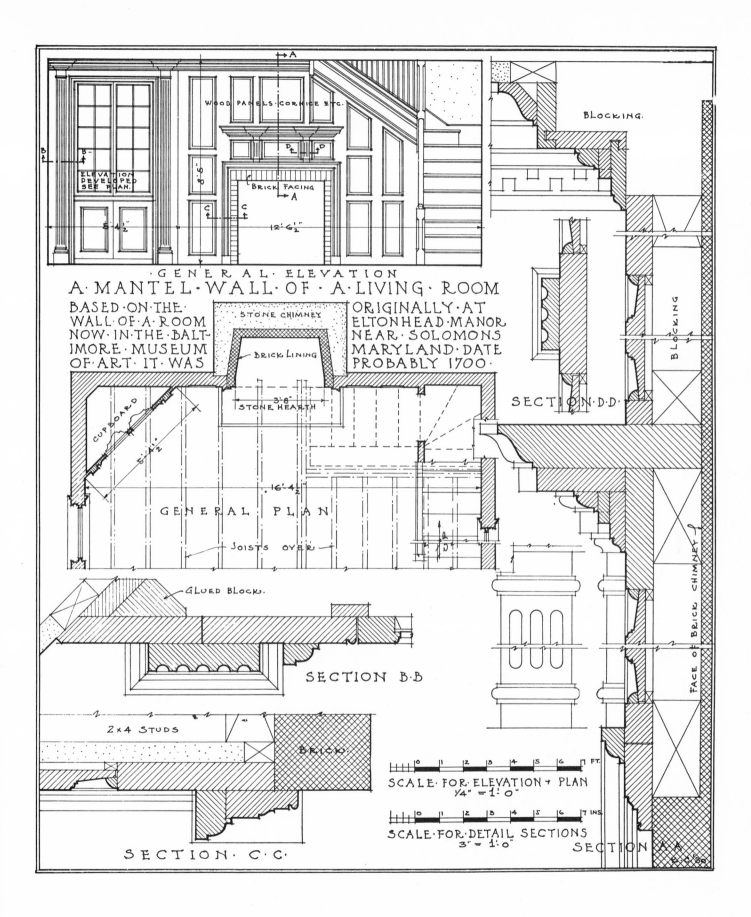

GENERAL·ELEVATION

A·MANTEL·WALL·OF·A·LIVING·ROOM

BASED·ON·THE·
WALL·OF·A·ROOM
NOW·IN·THE·BALT-
IMORE·MUSEUM
OF·ART·IT·WAS

ORIGINALLY·AT
ELTONHEAD·MANOR
NEAR·SOLOMONS
MARYLAND·DATE
PROBABLY·1700·

WOOD·PANELS·CORNICE·ETC.

ELEVATION
DEVELOPED
SEE·PLAN.

BRICK·FACING

8'·6"

12'·6½"

8'·4½"

STONE·CHIMNEY

BRICK·LINING

STONE·HEARTH

3'·8"

CUPBOARD

5'·4½"

16'·4½"

GENERAL·PLAN

JOISTS·OVER·

GLUED·BLOCK.

SECTION·B·B

2×4·STUDS

BRICK

SECTION·C·C·

BLOCKING.

SECTION·D·D·

BLOCKING

FACE·OF·BRICK·CHIMNEY

SCALE·FOR·ELEVATION·+·PLAN
¼"·=·1'·0"

SCALE·FOR·DETAIL·SECTIONS
3"·=·1'·0"

SECTION·A·A·

lies, deserves a better fate. One of the most pleasing features is the skillful junction of the two gambrel roofs. The lines are not parallel and the lower gambrel end is cut at the gable end in an unusual fashion. The small and very few dormers (or dormants, sleeping windows, as they are sometimes called by local carpenters) add character to the exterior but certainly not great comfort to the interior.

Surprising as it is to many not familiar with the houses of Maryland, the interiors of the large proportion of the houses, in spite of the small size of many of them, are often quite architectural. Some of the smallest houses boast at least one paneled room; where the detailing shows unmistakable evidences of the handicraft of workmen trained in old world traditions. Such a house is Eltonhead Manor House, built about 1690, which although it contained but six rooms, one of them is wainscoted from floor to ceiling, and shows a dentiled chairrail and cornice and a charming mantel of marked Queen Anne character. This room is now a part of the permanent collection of the Baltimore Art Museum.

Southern Maryland shows many more modest variations in wood of the traditional brick residence. These have the simple gable roof or gambrel with small and very few dormers. A characteristic trick of the chimneys is shown in Eltonhead. After the last fireplace, the chimney loses all contact with the house and rises in free and solitary height, eloquent of the early settlers fear of fire. These houses in early days were not painted, but after the Civil War, according to tradition, whitewash came into universal use as a method of cleaning up. Now these little white houses, usually inhabited by negroes, set back under old trees, have a rare charm

THE DOWER HOUSE, NEAR MARLBORO, PRINCE GEORGE COUNTY, MARYLAND

THE DOWER HOUSE,
LORD BALTIMORE'S
SHOOTING LODGE

ACTON—ANNE ARUNDEL COUNTY, MARYLAND, BUILT ABOUT 1790

and simple appeal, they are seldom but one room deep but often they extend in length, in varying heights, to five or six rooms.

Far from the houses already discussed and their socially homogeneous neighborhood, in Libertytown near Frederick in Western Maryland, is the charming old residence, built by Abraham Jones about 1798. The exterior bespeaks generous rooms and a gracious living, although the entrance door seems too narrow for its height and the iron rails are obviously a later addition. The interior stair spandrel shows an unusual radiating panel design and the newel seems one hundred years late, but examination fails to reveal any indication of its having been added.

All these houses are imbued with something of the same spirit and share a common quiet and modest dignity. They are of the very essence of old Maryland and silent reminders of the days and men that are gone. Those men—racy, hospitable, generous, alike in spirit and interests, proud, devoted to the good things of this world, built all of these qualities into their homes and undoubtedly agreed with Sir Henry Wotten in 1624 that:—

"Every man's proper Mansion House and Home, being the Theatre of his Hospitality, the Seat of his self Fruition, the comfortablest part of his own Life, the Noblest of his sons Inheritance, a kind of private Princedom; may, to the possessor thereof be an Epitomy of the whole World; may well deserve by these Attributes, according to the degree of the Master, to be decently and delightfully adorned."

STAIRWAY, THE JONES–SAPPINGTON HOUSE, LIBERTYTOWN,
FREDERICK COUNTY, MARYLAND

DETAIL SOUTHWEST ROOM—THE JAMES BRICE HOUSE, ANNAPOLIS, MARYLAND

MANTEL, SOUTH WEST ROOM

THE LIVING ROOM
THE JAMES BRICE HOUSE
ANNAPOLIS, MARYLAND

MEASURED DRAWINGS *from*
The George F. Lindsay Collection

DOORWAY, LIVING ROOM

MANTEL

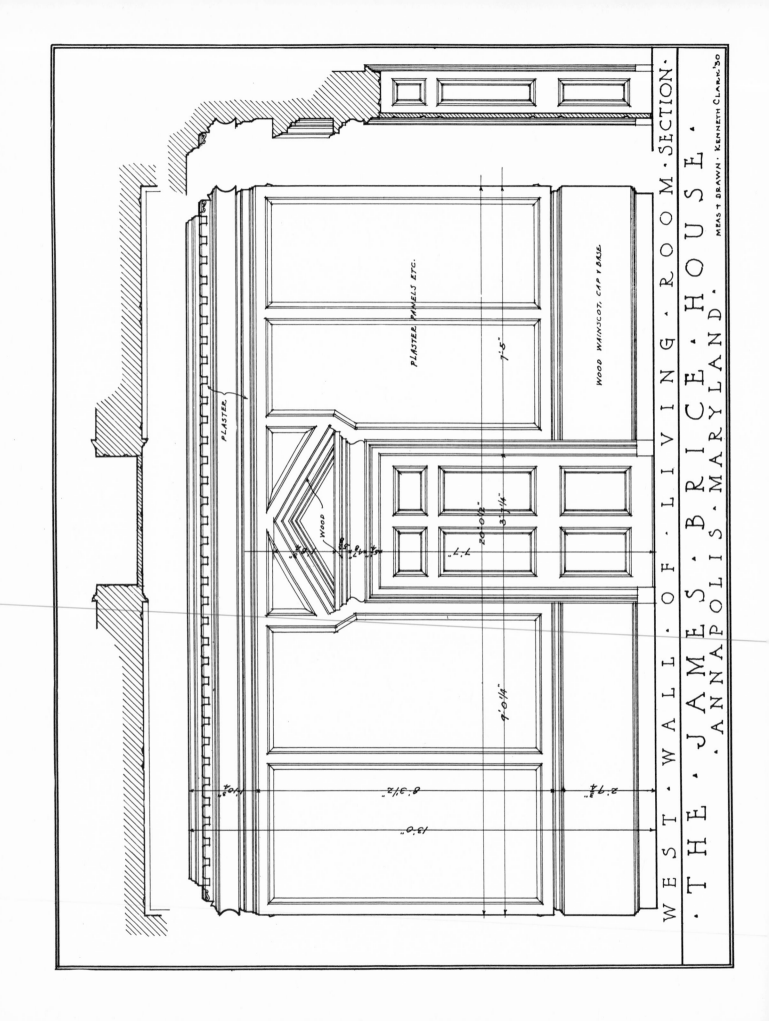

· W E S T · W A L L · O F · L I V I N G · R O O M · S E C T I O N ·

· T H E · J A M E S · B R I C E · H O U S E ·
· A N N A P O L I S · M A R Y L A N D ·

MEAS ϯ DRAWN · KENNETH CLARK '30

PLASTER. PANELS ETC.

WOOD WAINSCOT, CAP ϯ BASE

PLASTER.

WOOD

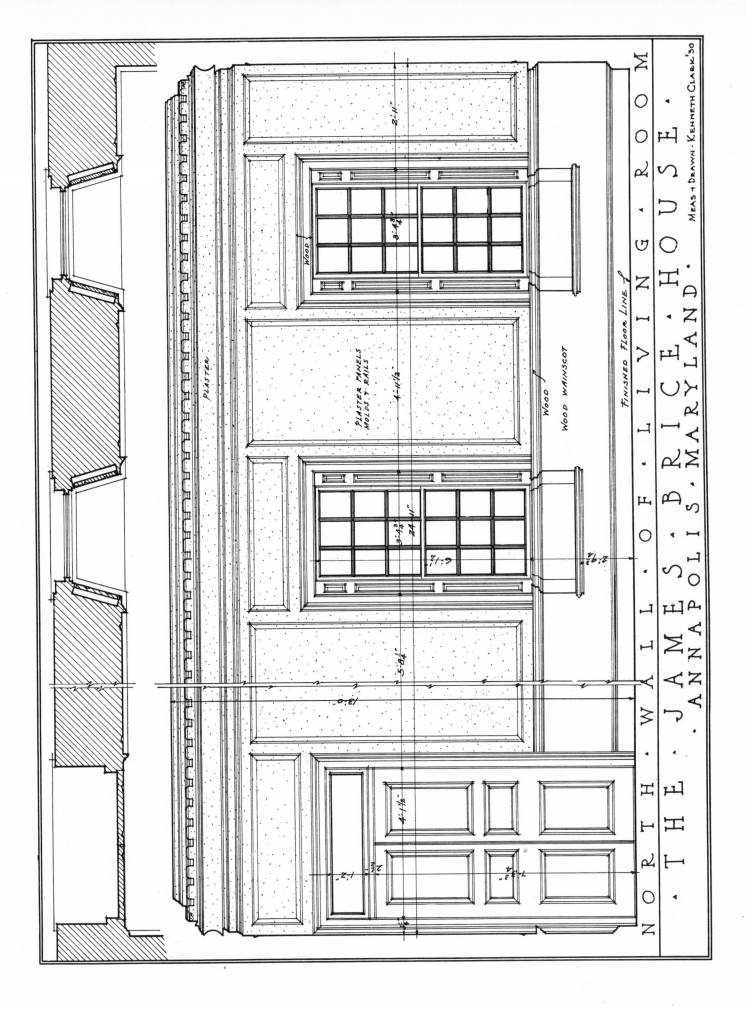

· N O R T H · W A L L · O F · L I V I N G · R O O M ·

· T H E · J A M E S · B R I C E · H O U S E ·
· A N N A P O L I S · M A R Y L A N D ·

MEAS + DRAWN · KENNETH CLARK '30

FINISHED FLOOR LINE

PLASTER PANELS
MOLDS. Y. RAILS

PLASTER

WOOD

WOOD WAINSCOT

THE JAMES BRICE HOUSE, BUILT IN 1740 AT ANNAPOLIS, MARYLAND

174

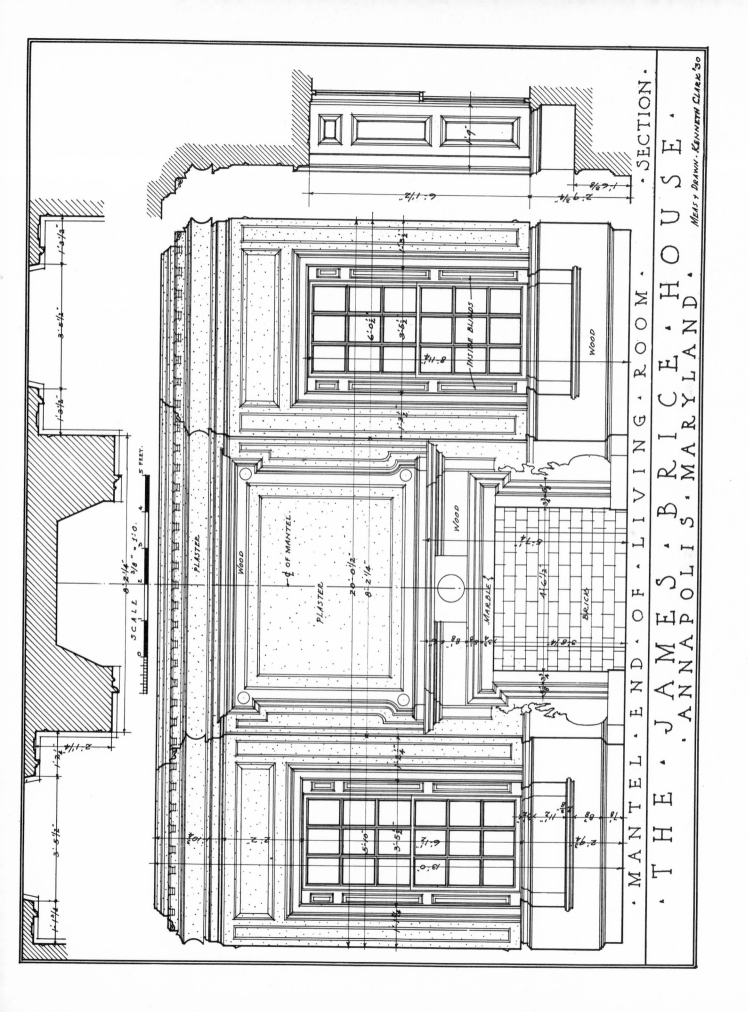

· MANTEL · END · OF · LIVING · ROOM · · SECTION ·

· THE · JAMES · BRICE · HOUSE ·
· ANNAPOLIS · MARYLAND ·

Meis * Drawn · Kenneth Clark '30

RECEPTION ROOM

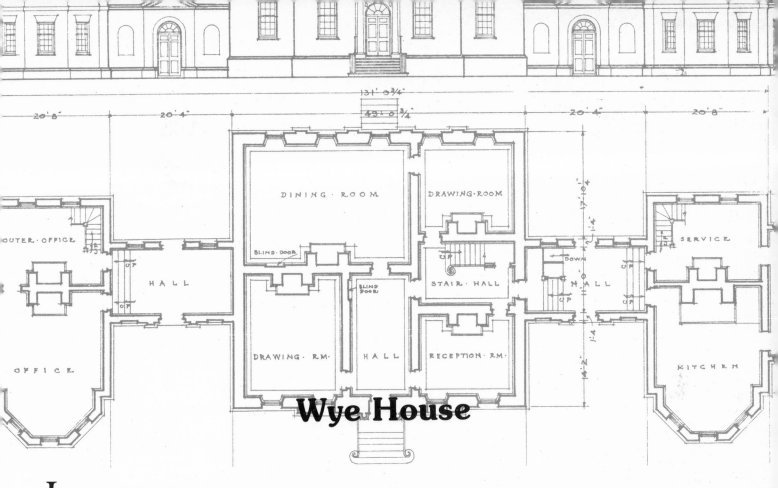

Wye House

In Talbot County, Maryland, situated on the westerly bank of the Front Wye River, and approximately midway between Easton and Clarebourne, is an estate which combines rare historic value with an architectural interest that places it in a class with the great residences of our early aristocratic land owners. To many, this great acreage is known as the Lloyds Estate, while others refer to the location as "Wye" House, the home of the Lloyds for eight generations.

Existing records tell us that Edward Lloyd the first came to the colony of Virginia from Wales in 1623 and was a burgess in the Virginia Assembly which met at "Preston-on-Patuxent" (Charlesgift). It was Edward Lloyd the first, who in 1662 built the original residence known as Wye House, upon a tract of land estimated to have been five thousand acres. Although this house stood for over one hundred years, there are no records whatsoever of it.

On the night of March 13, 1781, an incendiary fire burned the original Wye House and during the conflagration all of the historic records of the Lloyd family, the family treasures and plate disappeared. Only a small part of the original Wye House remained standing and today this is used as an outbuilding.

Available records indicate that the present Wye House was rebuilt by Edward Lloyd the fourth, immediately after the original house was destroyed. He succeeded in erecting a most charming colonial residence which seems to have been planned not only as a residence, but as a pivot or key building to a great es-

tate. Other features of the general plan followed in a most capable manner. An observer will note the careful arrangement of all the buildings.

Comparatively few sight-seers have visited Wye House, for the estate is not easily accessible and not open to the public. That may also account for the fact that Wye House is not well known to students of Colonial Architecture, except those who may reside in that particular locality. Furthermore, the casual tourist who may use the secondary roadway which passes its gates, will not see any part of Wye House or its buildings for the reason that they are set back approximately three-quarters of a mile from the roadway. One must be carefully directed to its location, which is marked by a pair of great wrought iron gates which were brought from Italy by a later Lloyd and erected as the entrance to this great estate. These gates are kept locked and bolted and this entry is no longer used. The driveway to Wye House has not been preserved and nature has converted it into a grassy lane that stretches away in the distance for nearly three-quarters of a mile. The sheep that are kept at Wye have wisely chosen what remains of this roadway as a pasturing place and, if one can for a moment forget its present appearance, the former grandeur and elegance of the main approach to Wye House can be appreciated. Magnificent trees still flank both sides of the roadway and form an arboreal passage worthy of Versailles. Entry to the estate is now made by a service roadway which passes the old slave quarters.

At the end of the main driveway stands the present

ENTRANCE PORCH—WYE HOUSE
Built in Talbot County, Maryland in 1782

PORCH DETAIL, REAR ELEVATION

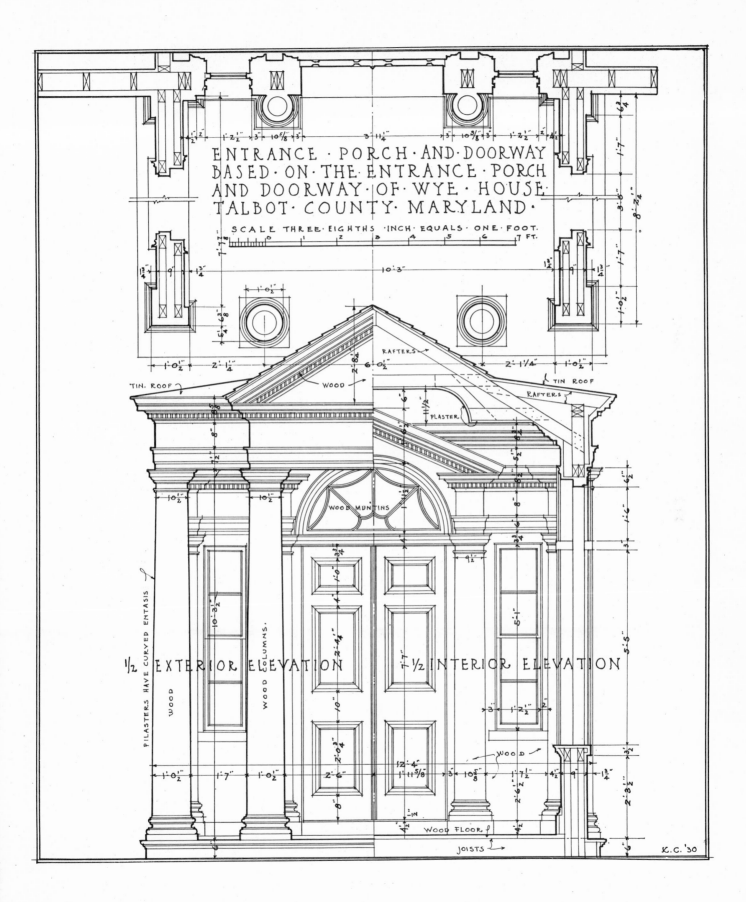

ENTRANCE · PORCH · AND · DOORWAY
BASED · ON · THE · ENTRANCE · PORCH
AND · DOORWAY · OF · WYE · HOUSE
TALBOT · COUNTY · MARYLAND ·

SCALE · THREE · EIGHTHS · INCH · EQUALS · ONE · FOOT.

½ EXTERIOR ELEVATION   7½ INTERIOR ELEVATION

PILASTERS HAVE CURVED ENTASIS

TIN ROOF
RAFTERS
WOOD
PLASTER
TIN ROOF
RAFTERS
WOOD MUNTINS
WOOD
WOOD COLUMNS.
WOOD
WOOD FLOOR
JOISTS

K.C. '30

FIRST WYE HOUSE, BUILT IN 1662—ONLY PART OF ORIGINAL HOUSE NOW STANDING

Wye House. This building is of two stories and includes a long hall from the entry porch to the porch on the rear, a drawing room, parlor, dining room and chambers. One story wings, connected by corridors, contain a library on one side and service rooms on the other. In all, it presents a pleasing facade of approximately two hundred feet. The exterior shows a simple and dignified treatment of siding with shuttered windows, except for the central three light window over the entrance porch which is ornamented by pilasters and entablature. The main roof, roofs of side wings and entrance porch were originally shingled but are now of slate, and in elevation are pediments of flush boarding retaining the same roof pitch throughout. The entrance motif consists of two columns and two pilasters on the front and flush boarding on the sides, pierced by circular headed openings. Stone steps, enclosed by hedges, complete this central motif. There is no carving on the exterior. In fact this simplicity of treatment is carried out in the interior of the house, where one still finds cornices,

arches, pilasters, architraves, panelling and trim of simple profiles. Charming mantels set off these rooms, though none of them contain more than a carved bead or fret. The doors are fitted with exquisite hardware in silver, brass and wrought iron that was undoubtedly made and brought from England. One cannot forget the furnishings of Wye House. The rooms are full of rare colonial furniture and pictures, vases and cameos, andirons and fireplace implements, lamps and candelabra, firearms and dozens of other things. There are many priceless framed parchments of great historic value and aside from its beauty as a colonial relic, Wye House is literally a museum. Fortunately, this fine collection of antiques has not been allowed to fall into the hands of collectors.

On the rear of the house is a colonnaded open porch facing a great rectangular lawn which in turn is enclosed on each side by beautiful boxwood hedges and trees that only age and good care could produce. At one end of the lawn and facing directly the rear of the house is the Orangery. To behold the Orangery from the porch in its frame of lawn, sky and trees at each side is to gaze at a picture perfect in its composition. The first impression to both layman and student of architecture is pleasing beyond words. Invariably a closer inspection is desired and one walks down the great lawn to examine what may easily be considered a perfect example of Georgian design. The building is unusual in its simplicity and perfection. It is two stories flanked on both sides by one story wings of equal proportions. The roofs are shingled. The lower half of the two story center is rusticated stonework. Rusticated stone quoins continue on the corners to the roof. One will receive a great surprise to discover that what seems to be four flat arches with wedge-shaped voussoirs over the four large windows are nothing more than wood lintels, hewn and carved to carry out the treatment of stone rustications below. Time and weather have almost succeeded in blending these wood lintels into the general color of the building. The upper story is of brick, stuccoed, and the side wings are of the same materials. The beauty of this building reveals the work of a great architect and the cooperation of capable craftsmen.

As far as is known, the Orangery was built shortly after the present Wye House and was used to house plants and shrubs during the winter months. Since that time, the Orangery has served many purposes principally that of storehouse. Without a doubt, this building is unsurpassed in this country and should be preserved as an historic example of Georgian Architecture.

The interest of Wye House, which tends to increase from the moment of passing the front gates and seems to have reached its peak after seeing the Orangery, is not at an end. There still remains the family burying plot, the last resting place of the Lloyds who have passed on during the three centuries that have elapsed. This is located at the rear of the Orangery. In a book called *"Historic Graves of Maryland and the District of Columbia"* by Helen W. Ridgeley, the author gives an interesting account of the Wye burial plot, which begins by saying: "On account of its age and of the prominent people buried there and also because of the beauty of its tombs and their quaint inscriptions, the old Lloyd burying ground at Wye, the home of the Lloyds since 1660, is the most interesting in Maryland . . . . . . The family

SOUTH FAÇADE

181

PARLOR

HALL

badge of a lion rampant, appears on variously carved shields." Here also are the unmarked graves of those who died and were buried before Col. Philemon Lloyd, who died in 1685. His is the oldest stone with the exception of one inscribed to the memory of Capt. Strong of Stephney, in the County of Middlesex, who died in 1684. There are no records available of the Lloyd connection to Captain Strong. Close to Col. Philemon Lloyd, is buried his wife who died in 1697 and his three daughters. Much can be written about those buried at Wye, particularly the historically famous members of the family who died in the service of their country and who are now recorded in the archives of our history.

There are other interesting buildings and quaint details. There are the "Smoke" House and the old slave quarters and more recent additions, all comprising a small village in itself. One can still see the colored folk going quietly about their chores, the major part of which consists of caring for the grounds and landscaping around the house and Orangery. A rare old U shaped brick gutter leads away from the house. Last, but not least, are the brick walls enclosing the gardens and burial plot. These are of handmade brick with sloping copings of the same material. The walls are pierced by arched openings where paths occur. Covered with vines and moss, and overhung by trees, these walls help complete the perfect picture.

There are few estates in America today which exemplify the complete requirements necessary to the conduct of what was a community in itself. Mt. Vernon is one and Wye House another. They were self-sustaining in almost every particular and both have the various outbuildings which the many trades and crafts required. Wye House can teach us much of the life lived by its early owners who combined culture with the rugged determination on which was built the foundations of our present government.

SIDE ELEVATION WITH UNIQUE GUTTER

SOUTH FAÇADE

DINING ROOM

DRAWING ROOM FROM DINING ROOM

MANTEL,
DRAWING
ROOM

ESCUTCHEON AND HANDLE—FIRST FLOOR DOORS

ESCUTCHEON AND KNOB—SLIDING DOORS, FIRST FLOOR

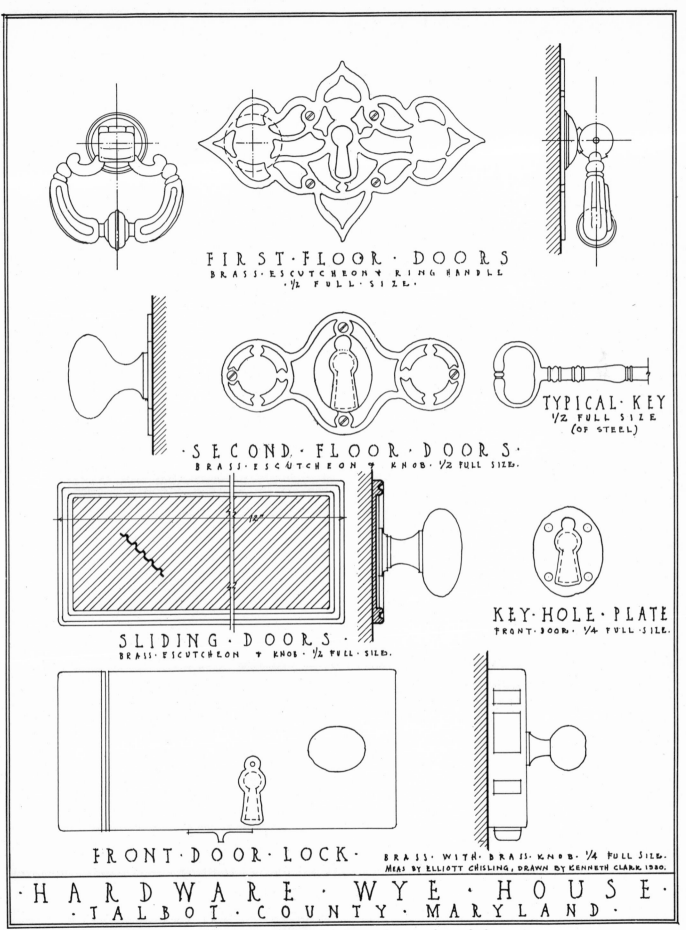

FIRST·FLOOR·DOORS
BRASS·ESCUTCHEON + RING HANDLE
·½ FULL·SIZE·

TYPICAL·KEY
½ FULL SIZE
(OF STEEL)

SECOND·FLOOR·DOORS·
BRASS·ESCUTCHEON + KNOB· ½ FULL SIZE·

SLIDING·DOORS·
BRASS·ESCUTCHEON + KNOB· ½ FULL·SIZE·

KEY·HOLE·PLATE
FRONT·DOOR· ¼ FULL·SIZE·

FRONT·DOOR·LOCK· BRASS· WITH·BRASS·KNOB· ¼ FULL·SIZE·
MEAS BY ELLIOTT CHISLING, DRAWN BY KENNETH CLARK 1930·

HARDWARE · WYE · HOUSE·
·TALBOT·COUNTY·MARYLAND·

Drawings are reproduced exactly at scale marked

STAIR DETAIL

INTERIOR DOORWAY

ORANGERY
WYE HOUSE, TALBOT COUNTY
MARYLAND

MEASURED DRAWINGS *from*
The George F. Lindsay Collection

SOUTH FAÇADE

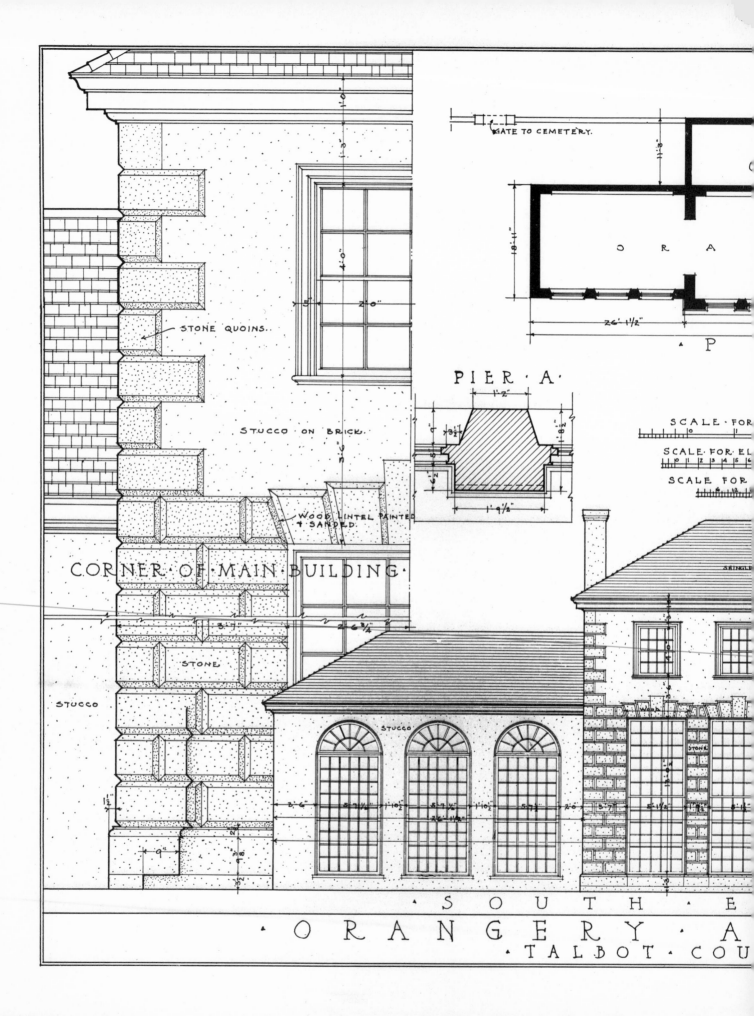

GATE TO CEMETERY.

PIER · A ·

STONE QUOINS.

STUCCO ON BRICK.

WOOD LINTEL PAINTED & SANDED.

CORNER · OF · MAIN · BUILDING ·

STONE

STUCCO

STUCCO

SCALE · FOR
SCALE · FOR · EL
SCALE · FOR

· S O U T H · E
· O R A N G E R Y · A
· T A L B O T · C O U

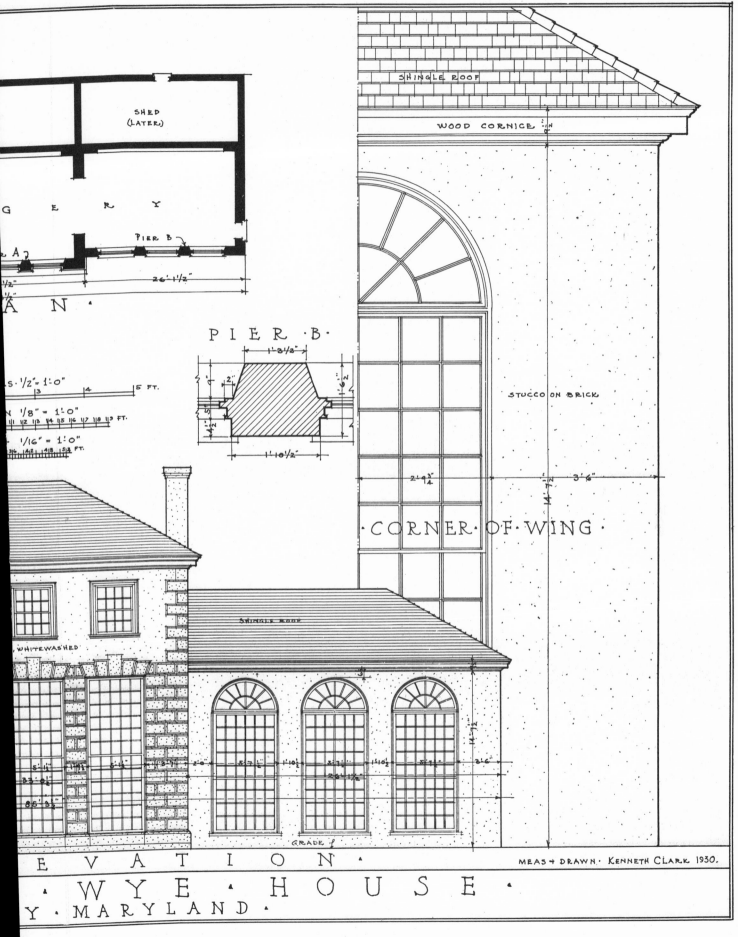

SHED
(LATER)

G E R Y

PIER B

A

26'-1½"

N

s. ½" = 1'0"

N ⅛" = 1'0"

1/16" = 1'0"

P I E R · B ·

1'-3½"

1'-10½"

SHINGLE ROOF

WOOD · CORNICE · ON

STUCCO ON BRICK

3'-6"

CORNER · OF · WING ·

WHITEWASHED

SHINGLE ROOF

GRADE

E V A T I O N ·

MEAS + DRAWN · KENNETH CLARK 1930.

· W Y E · H O U S E ·

Y · M A R Y L A N D ·

PORTRAIT OF MATTHEW BUCKLAND, ARCHITECT

Painted by Peale for Matthias Hammond

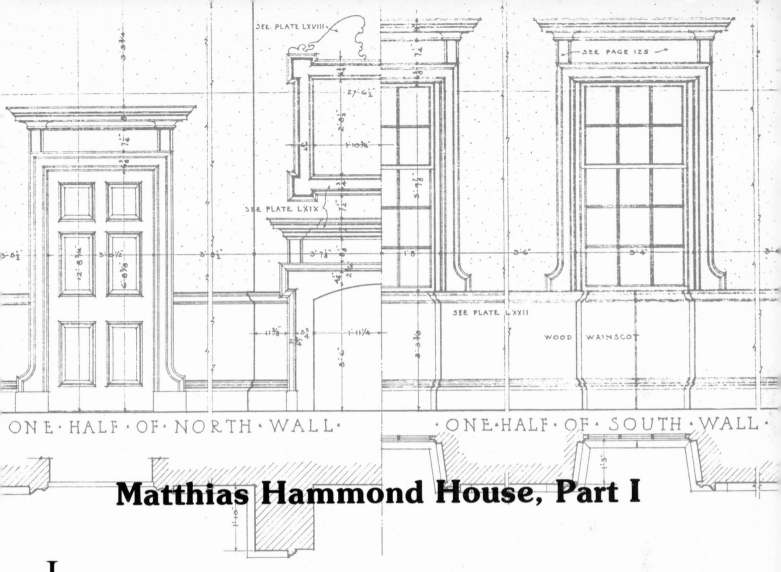

· O N E · H A L F · O F · N O R T H · W A L L ·   · O N E · H A L F · O F · S O U T H · W A L L ·

Matthias Hammond House, Part I

I**T IS NOT STRANGE** that Annapolis, the capital of the State of Maryland, should bear stamped unmistakably upon its ancient buildings the image of the highest Georgian standards of the Architecture of the mother country, England, for this "Colonial" city was perhaps more intimately related to and kept in closer touch with its national progenitor than any other on this continent. Its people were substantial, wealthy and aristocratic, their thoughts and actions bespoke England rather than the rugged infant nucleus that was one day destined to become this United States of America. The Annopolitans of the 18th century were not hard fisted pioneers, fighting a wilderness for a precarious existence, but rather the finished result of those pioneers' efforts, a settled community of sophisticated citizens, living an English life in everything but locale.

They had their theatres and clubs, their servants and their coaches and fours; among them were lawyers, doctors and architects. The professions were liberally practiced and the rich men of the colony could afford to use such service. Indeed wealth in this city was almost up to the later standards set by our captains of industry, for men like Charles Carroll and others were owners of substantial businesses and properties that today would dub them by that title. Such citizens were

content with nothing but the best things in life and the houses they built to live in were a reflection of their condition and their age.

In 1770, Matthias Hammond, a lawyer and planter, being interested in taking to himself a mate to share his fortune and his home, began construction of perhaps one of the best examples of domestic architecture of the period.

He engaged as architect one Matthew Buckland who hailed, tradition says, from Philadelphia and who was efficient enough to impress upon his client the substantial merit of his work; that he was appreciated there is definite evidence for his portrait painted by Peale and executed at the order of Hammond was destined to grace the walls of his masterpiece for many years, and hangs there today mute evidence that his genius carved for itself a niche well worthy of commemoration.

Evidences of his command of design are strongly apparent elsewhere in Annapolis, but the Hammond house is the culmination of his efforts and stands today as one of the finest, if not the finest, example of the work of the Colonial Period.

Situated on the corner at the crossing of King George Street and Maryland Avenue, the house occupies a block front and the outer dimensions of its plan are ap-

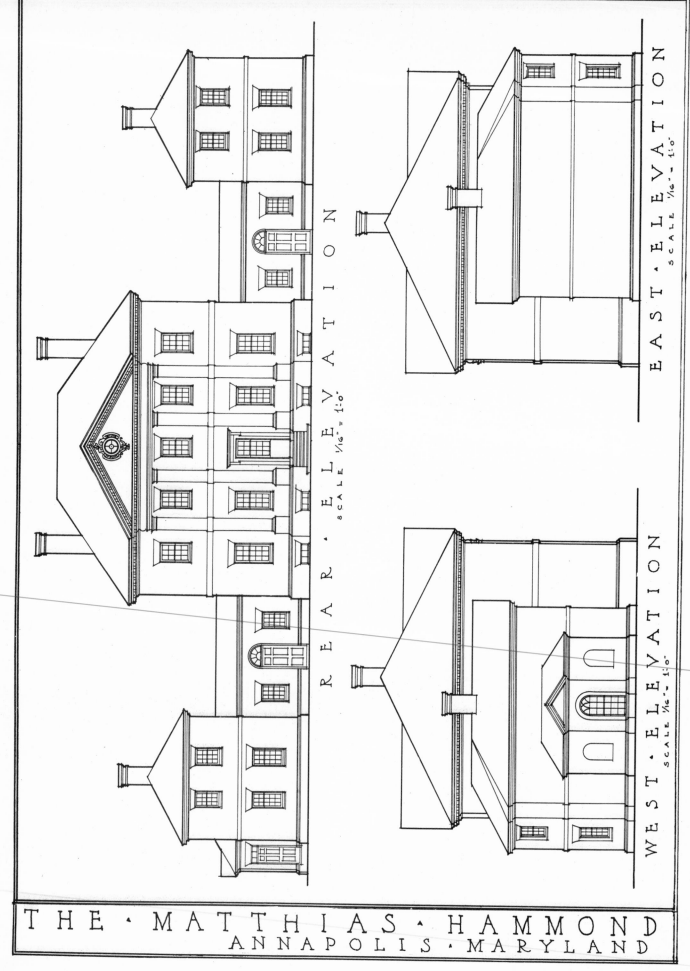

EAST · ELEVATION
SCALE ¹⁄₁₆" = 1'·0"

REAR · ELEVATION
SCALE ¹⁄₁₆" = 1'·0"

WEST · ELEVATION
SCALE ¹⁄₁₆" = 1'·0"

THE · MATTHIAS · HAMMOND
ANNAPOLIS · MARYLAND

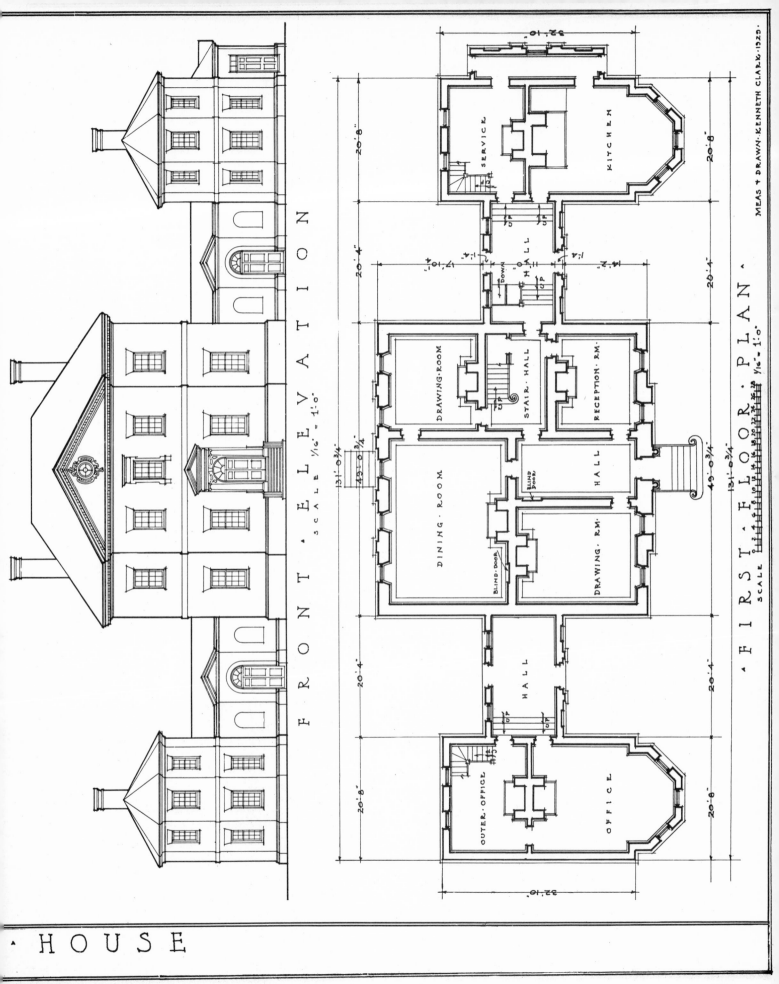

· H O U S E ·

F R O N T · E L E V A T I O N

SCALE ¹⁄₁₆" = 1'·0"

· F I R S T · F L O O R · P L A N ·

SCALE ¹⁄₁₆" = 1'·0"

MEAS + DRAWN. KENNETH CLARK. 1925.

SERVICE

KITCHEN

HALL

DRAWING·ROOM

STAIR·HALL

RECEPTION·RM.

DINING·ROOM

HALL

BLIND·DOOR

DRAWING·RM.

OUTER·OFFICE

HALL

OFFICE

proximately 131 feet x 46 feet. The facade presents a two story main house and wings connected by one story links. Its principal exterior characteristics are dignity and simplicity relieved by the elaborate and beautifully carved wood doorway with window over, a cornice and pediment window. The ornament is concentrated in these details and thereby serves to accentuate the massiveness of the large areas of brickwork. The lintels are flat brick arches and the base or water table is of moulded brick. The band course between first and second story windows and the water table have been laid with practically no joint, in contrast with the rest of the wall surfaces and the lack of the vertical lines in those members gives them a horizontality that was undoubtedly a deliberate and foreseen result of the architect's study. The brick units average 8″ x 4″ x 2⅝″ and the joints, of white mortar, are not more than ¼″ in thickness. An interesting detail, that seems to give quite a "sparkle" to the texture of the walls, is the fact that the mason after striking the joint practically flush has drawn a line, evidently using a straight edge and his trowel point, in the middle of each joint, both horizontal and vertical and this treatment tends to eliminate the apparentness of many irregularities caused by variations in the brick shapes. The chimneys are square in plan and are topped out with a simple brick coping. The window reveals are uniformly 4″ and in the central bay of the front elevation the additional thickness of wall required for the break has been added to the window frame outside, making the inside reveal, which comes in the same room as a window in the thinner wall, the same.

The brick is rich, dull salmon in color, laid in Flemish bond and the present surface texture is about that of the usual run of modern unselected "common."

The garden—or rear—facade follows the front identically as to general proportions, but the main house is broken by a treatment of four brick pilasters with a full cornice, frieze and architrave of wood above them and the pediment and its decorated window is repeated.

The plan has many clever and ingenious features. The right hand wing, looking from the street, is a kitchen and service portion and the left hand one, an office wing for the original owner's use. This wing does not connect with the main house by an interior door, but is entered only through the link by the front and the garden doors.

The main house plan is unconventional in many ways, but is a finished architectural study with all axes, etc., so necessary to the success of a formal, symmetrical

house of this type, properly considered and worked out. The stairway, contrary to the usual procedure, is not made a feature of the entrance hall, but is relegated to one side in a separate space, leaving the entrance hall a perfectly symmetrical room as to openings, etc. A door opens directly opposite the front door into the "big" room of the house, called the "State Dining Room" and is on axis with the door to the garden. The uses of the minor rooms are doubtful. They have been marked on the plan, as "Drawing Room" and "Reception Room." It is possible that the rear "Drawing Room" served the family as Dining Room on other than "State" occasions, but nothing warrants this conclusion except its location. Perhaps life in this mansion made every meal a ceremony, whether attended by guests or

not and worthy of the magnificent setting the State Dining Room provides. The treatment of the minor rooms on the first floor is simple, each has a fine mantel, wainscot and cornice, each room treated individually without repetition of design.

The woodwork of the interiors of this house is its most remarkable feature. The use of the material and its ornamental treatment by the architect and his craftsmen are worthy of separate consideration.

The second floor plan repeats the first exactly as to spaces, the room over the State Dining Room being a Ball Room treated in an Adamesque style with a garlanded mantel and fluted cornice with urn ornaments at intervals. The space above the second floor ceiling is not finished off, but left merely as an attic ventilated

Detail of Link between Main House and Wing

STREET FACADE

Detail of Entablature—Main Entrance Doorway

STREET FACADE—*Detail of Main Entrance*

MEASURED DRAWINGS *from*
The George F. Lindsay Collection

SCALE DETAIL OF FRONT DOOR

MEAS & DRAWN KENNETH CLARK '23.

·THE·MATTHIAS·HAMMOND·HOUSE·
·ANNAPOLIS·MARYLAND·

STREET FACADE—
Detail of Second Story Hall Window

by the two pediment windows, which relieved the architect from the necessity of breaking the roof with dormers, the absence of which helps the repose and simplicity of the elevations.

On the West wall of the main house is an arched window, lighting the stair hall, which is treated with a quoined trim that appears rather heavy in contrast with the delicacy of the other details.

The whole exterior scheme seems wonderfully consistent and logical. The method of linking wings and main house by passages opening on both the street and garden front gives access to the servants' portion and the office wing without disturbing the occupants of the main house. Formerly, when the Hammond property was of far greater compass than the present lot, the rear elevation looked out upon a garden of generous proportions. The only remainder of this former grandure is some fine box, which now grows almost on the line of a neighboring house that in these surroundings shocks by its modern utilitarian ugliness.

In the height of its glory the Hammond House was a true example of an American gentleman's home where he lived a life of refinement, surrounded by a setting that could do nothing but itensify the spirit of hospitality and good will that flowed within its walls. It stands today a living example of great architecture that we who run and rush may read and absorb some of its beauties and the methods by which they were achieved. "Modern" movements may come and go but such work as this is never old or new. It stands, as all the classics of our arts stand, self sufficient and complete.

GARDEN FACADE—*Detail of Central Bay*

GARDEN FACADE

GARDEN FACADE—

Detail of Pediment and Cartouche

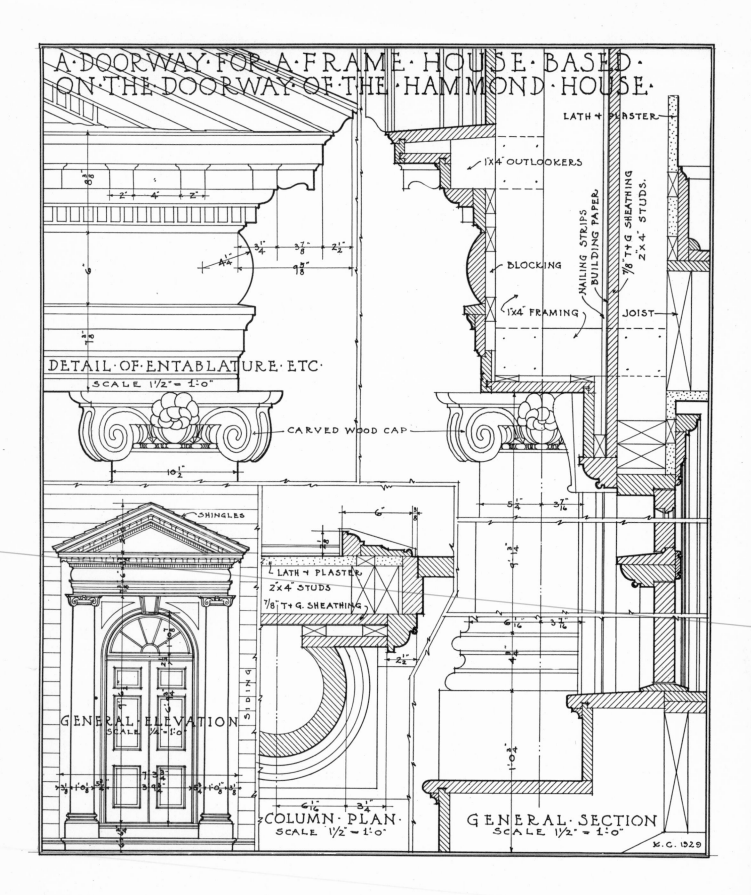

A·DOORWAY·FOR·A·FRAME·HOUSE·BASED·
ON·THE·DOORWAY·OF·THE·HAMMOND·HOUSE.

DETAIL·OF·ENTABLATURE·ETC.
SCALE 1½" = 1:0"

CARVED WOOD CAP

LATH + PLASTER

1X4 OUTLOOKERS

BLOCKING

1X4 FRAMING

NAILING STRIPS
BUILDING PAPER.

7/8" T+G SHEATHING
2"X4" STUDS.

JOIST

SHINGLES

LATH + PLASTER
2x4" STUDS
7/8" T+G. SHEATHING

SIDING

GENERAL·ELEVATION
SCALE ¼" = 1:0"

COLUMN·PLAN.
SCALE 1½" = 1:0"

GENERAL·SECTION
SCALE 1½" = 1:0"

K.C. 1929

Garden Doorway

Detail of Entablature—Garden Doorway

ENTRANCE HALL—MATTHEW BUCKLAND, ARCHITECT

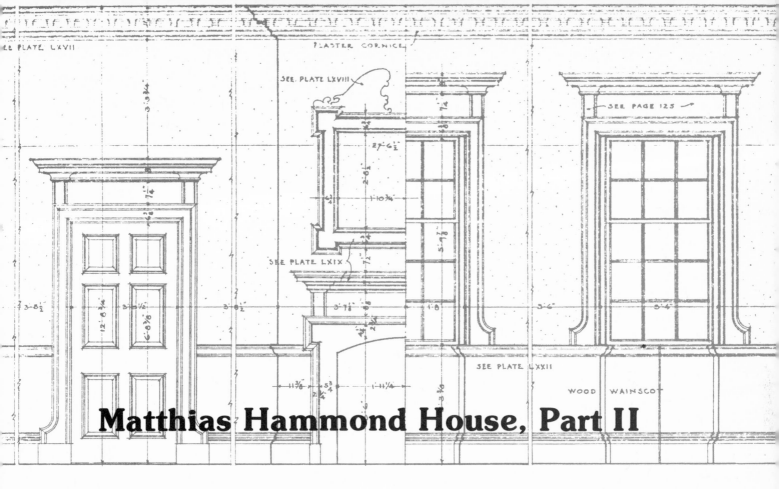

Matthias Hammond House, Part II

THE HAMMOND-HARWOOD HOUSE adds
much to the charm of old Annapolis, which grows with
every visit. True, many of the minor houses there are
of the pre-Civil War period when the increasing needs
of the Naval Academy necessitated more buildings in
the town. Simple and purely utilitarian, they afford a
satisfactory setting for the eight superb eighteenth century houses which remain to bear eloquent testimony
to the love of the beautiful which existed there during
the trying days preceding the American Revolution.
Annapolitans justly take pride in the fact that three of
these great mansions were lived in by signers of the
Declaration of Independence, Charles Carroll, Samuel
Chase, and William Paca.

The house we are discussing was built by Matthias
Hammond, a most active Son of Liberty and leader in
the patriot cause. What a contrast here to the political
attitude in the northern cities where the members of the
wealthy class, with few exceptions, either remained Tory,
and later paid the penalty thereof, or took little active
part in the proceedings which led to the birth of our
republic!

The architect of the Hammond-Harwood house was
one Matthew Buckland. Tradition says he was a Phila-
delphian, but little evidence of that beautiful colonial
style of architecture so peculiar to Philadelphia is to
be noted in his work here. We do know, however, that
he was introduced to one of the Carrolls of Annapolis
by George Mason of Gunston Hall.

Possibly no other house in America shows so clearly
how our eighteenth century architects worked. These
men took the styles of the old world, adapted them to
local conditions, as a rule simplified them in keeping
with the simpler background here, and in thus doing
evolved a style of their own, which we are justly proud
to call American. They rarely slavishly copied the designs which came to them from across the water in the
splendid English eighteenth century books of architecture. They accepted the fundamentals, but generally
changed the details according to their own fancies.

Let us throw ourselves back into the period of the
designing of the house and imagine ourselves in Buckland's office. Charles Willson Peale gave us the atmosphere in the background of his portrait of Buckland.
There we see plaster casts, the base of a Doric column,
the façade of a Corinthian temple. On the table in front
of the sitter are some architectural books, his draught-
ing tools and the completed ground plan of this house.
We can be sure that Buckland either owned or had access to those great English elephant folios filled with
beautifully engraved plates, whose publication was made
possible by advance subscriptions from the nobility
and gentlemen of England. Imagine his delight at the
receipt of an order which would allow full scope to his
learning and imagination. We can see him poring over
the pages of that splendid large folio, "*A Book of Architecture*," by James Gibbs, London 1728. In *Plate 64*
he finds a pedimented house with two wings attached,
the general lines of which he believes will meet the requirements of his wealthy client. Here is to be his gen-

Showing wood stairway, wainscot, floors, balustrade, etc.

eral scheme. The columnated passageways which attach the wings to the house do not quite meet his approval. They are over ornate. He substitutes for these simple one-story pedimented fronts, which are much less ornate than the façade of the main portion of the house. In the Gibbs plan, the wings are square and uninteresting. For these Buckland substitutes those beautiful octagonal walls, so much in vogue in England in the Adam period—a change which emphasizes the classic beauty of the central portion. Buckland evidently was a man who kept himself up to date in architectural styles.

He becomes fascinated by the bull's eye windows in many of Gibbs' pediments. The cartouches interest him. In *Plate 110* he finds a bull's eye window the framing of which is the prototype of the one in this house. Here we find the same banded laurel wreath and the same heavy gougings at the side. The shape, in order to fit the opening, needs some adaptation. This he accomplishes by a simplification of the foliage on the sides and a change of certain details of the ornament at top and bottom. Interesting details are the whorls which Mr. Clark's telephoto lens clearly brings out in high relief. The quoined windows in *Plates 37 and 65* of Gibbs' also catch his eye and probably offer the suggestion for his window, which lights the stairway.

The doorway is called the most beautiful colonial doorway in America. The banded laurel below the pediment and of the lintel of the window just over it, and on one mantel might well have been taken from illustrations in another of Buckland's books, (we assume he owned them), "*The Designs of Inigo Jones*" by William Kent, London 1727. From *Plates 56 and 63* Buckland would have been able to obtain the arabesques and peculiar barbaric bird's heads he used in the friezes of the mantelpiece and the doorways in the beautiful dining room he built for Hammond.

One of the books on architecture freely advertised in our colonial news sheets was Abraham Swan's "*British Architect,*" published in London in 1745. In it we find a drawing of the magnificent cornice which Buckland followed in detail in designing the cornice of the grand dining room. An interesting feature of Buckland's cornice is the variety of rosettes placed between the modillions. One cannot help but marvel at the elaborately carved inside window shutters with their delicate "starfish rosettes" set in alternating octagonal and rounded coffers with carved egg and dart borders.

STAIR HALL—SECOND FLOOR

211

DETAIL OF
CORNICE—
THE BALL ROOM

MANTEL AND
CORNICE DETAILS

The carving on the chair-rail is equally noteworthy, as is also the ornamental moulding on the top of the base board, both of which are in thorough keeping with the rich ornament of the mantel, doorways, and doors of this more than remarkable room.

The Adam movement, as we know, gained little foothold in America until after the Revolution. However, in the Hammond-Harwood house, distinct traces of it are to be found. The bead and reel motive used in the door frames is a dominating note in the great work by Robert Adam on *"The Ruin of the Palace of the Emperor Diocletian at Spalatro in Dalmatia,"* 1764. The gouged motives in the lintel of the door frames may well have been suggested by this beautifully engraved volume, which had such an immediate effect upon English architecture. Other Adam motives which may have been the result of a study of the plates of this monumental volume are the spiral bandings on the dining room door frames and mouldings of the baseboard.

The ball room above the dining room can certainly be classed as early Adam. The frieze beneath the cornice is composed of a row of Adam vases separated from each other by six beaded channels. The oval rosettes at the ends of the mantelpiece, motives often used in the architecture and furniture are of the Adam period; also the bow knots of ribbon from which hang an elaborately carved garland of roses similiar to those found in the works of Adam's predecessors.

The interiors of the wings of the house are of great interest. The one on the west was and is the kitchen. It is practically the only restoration in the house.

Among other numerous interesting architectural details in various parts of the house is the placing of a Neptune's trident on the keystone arch of the window which lights the hall way.

It is more than likely that Buckland made his drawing for the mantel for the little room off the dining room from some in the book of Inigo Jones, who freely used the panelled block centered between bands of superimposed laurel leaves. To this design,

KITCHEN—WEST WING

MANTEL IN FRONT DRAWING ROOM

however, Buckland added to the border mouldings in the framing of the fire place that same bead and reel so often used by the architect of the Temple of Diocletian.

Color, that dominant note of eighteenth century interiors, is seen at its best in the pale green walls of the dining room, and in the gray blue walls of the ball room. On each side of the Peale portrait of Buckland in the dining room hang full length paintings by Wollaston of the Mr. and Mrs. Edmund Jennings who built the beautiful Brice house, another of the treasures belonging to St. John's College.

The Chippendale chairs and Sheraton sideboard belonged to early owners of the house. Much of the furniture is of Maryland origin. All of it shows a high excellence of workmanship and tells the story of the art of the cabinet maker in America.

The window drapings follow the styles of our early upholsterers. Red and yellow bourettes add great interest to the small rooms on each side of the entrance hall and an eighteenth century green damask decorates the windows of the small room off the dining room. In the ball room extraordinary India curtains painted in the beautiful colors of the Orient and in the pattern of the tree of life are reminiscent of the days when the Annapolis newspaper reported the frequent arrival of ships ladened with "European and East Indian merchandise." The toiles de Jouy in the bedrooms with the designs of the "Four Quarters of the Globe" and "America's Homage to France" are of the kind which might well have been sent back to Annapolis by the French officers who enjoyed its hospitality while quartered there during the winter after Yorktown.

Surely St. John's College, the third oldest educational institution in this country, has in this building a great laboratory of American art where students can be given some knowledge of the cultural things of life.

DETAIL OF MANTEL—FRONT DRAWING ROOM

THE GRAND DINING ROOM—NORTH WALL.

The GRAND DINING ROOM of
THE MATTHIAS HAMMOND HOUSE
ANNAPOLIS, MARYLAND

MEASURED DRAWINGS *from*
The George F. Lindsay Collection

THE GRAND DINING ROOM—SOUTH WALL

CORNICE OF DINING ROOM

DINING ROOM

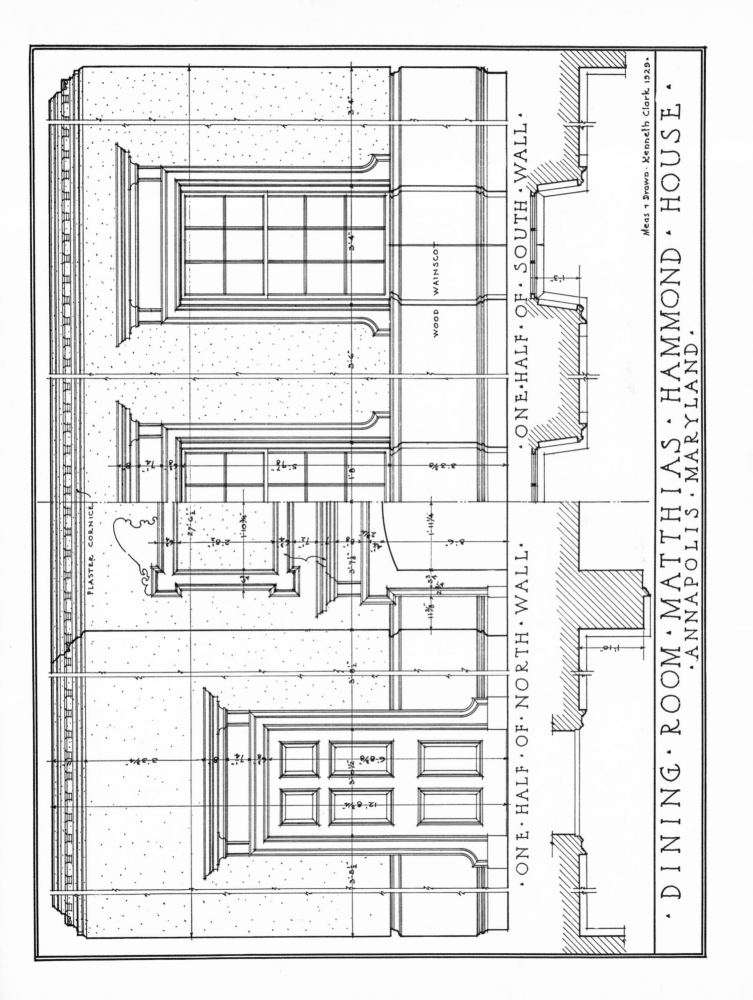

· DINING · ROOM · MATTHIAS · HAMMOND · HOUSE ·
· ANNAPOLIS · MARYLAND ·

· ONE · HALF · OF · SOUTH · WALL ·

· ONE · HALF · OF · NORTH · WALL ·

Meas & Drawn · Kenneth Clark · 1929 ·

WOOD WAINSCOT

PLASTER CORNICE

MANTEL DETAIL

MANTEL IN DINING ROOM

DETAIL OF DOOR HEAD

MANTEL DETAIL, DINING ROOM

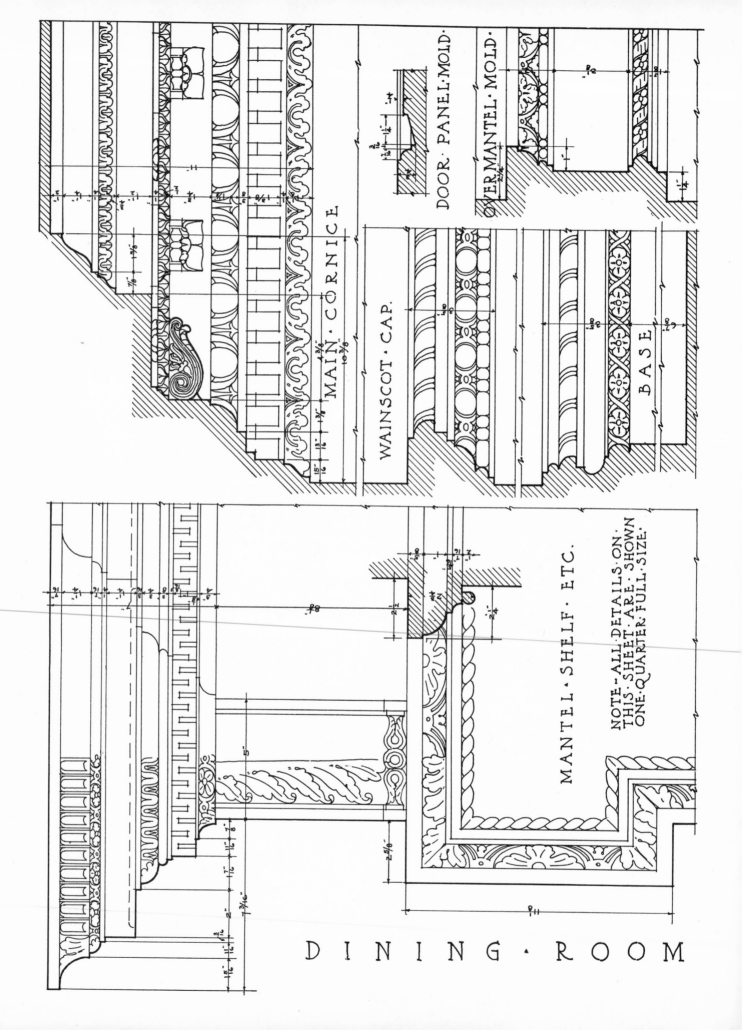

MAIN·CORNICE

WAINSCOT·CAP.

DOOR·PANEL·MOLD·

OVER·MANTEL·MOLD·

BASE

MANTEL·SHELF·ETC.

NOTE·ALL·DETAILS·ON·
THIS·SHEET·ARE·SHOWN
ONE·QUARTER·FULL·SIZE·

D I N I N G · R O O M

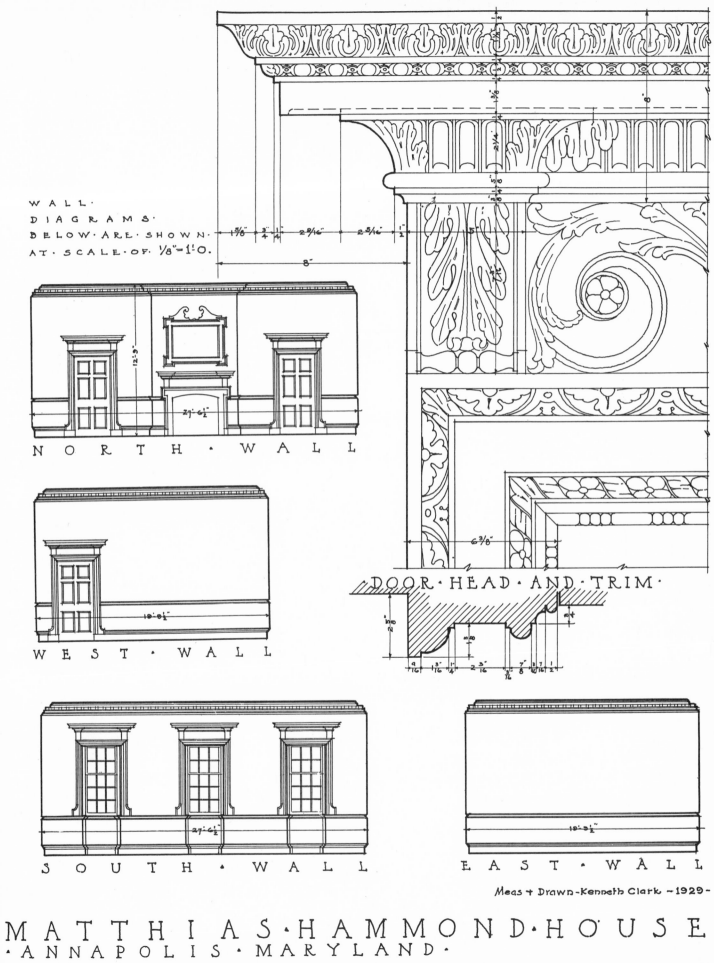

WALL·
DIAGRAMS·
BELOW·ARE·SHOWN·
AT·SCALE·OF·⅛"=1'·0.

NORTH·WALL

WEST·WALL

DOOR·HEAD·AND·TRIM·

SOUTH·WALL

EAST·WALL

Meas + Drawn - Kenneth Clark ~ 1929 ~

M A T T H I A S · H A M M O N D · H O U S E
· A N N A P O L I S · M A R Y L A N D ·